BUY TO LET
Loose

BUY TO LET
Loose

ANSHU KOTAK

THE MOMENTUM PUBLISHING COMPANY

First published in 2018 in the United Kingdom by
The Momentum Publishing Company

Copyright © Anshu Kotak 2018

First printing, 2018

ISBN: 978-1-911475-37-8

A CIP catalogue record for this book
is available from the British Library

Book cover by Hamish Braid
Inside illustration by Nishma Kotak
Typeset by Octavo Smith Publishing Services
Printed & bound by Opolgraf

www.buytoletloose.com

Thank you to my father, an incredibly talented architect that continues to provide invaluable guidance throughout my journey.

And to my mother, who by investing the family savings in property to generate more income became my inspiration.

Find enclosed a roadmap to financial freedom
& begin your journey...

CONTENTS

ABOUT THE AUTHOR

In Order to Enjoy the Five Senses,
a Sixth Is Often Needed: Money

I started dancing at fifteen. My passion for dance took over by the age of seventeen when I turned semi-professional and performed in concerts and shows across the UK and Europe. I felt torn. I searched for a university undergraduate program in the UK where I could combine mathematics & dance, the two subjects I felt blessed to be naturally good at, but alas, it 'made sense' for me to academically pursue maths at The London School of Economics (LSE) and recreationally pursue dance in my spare time.

My first year at university found me skipping lectures to go for auditions. I didn't think it was that big of a deal until I got my first-year grade, a 3rd. I realised I wasn't doing either path justice and so I decided to take a somewhat unorthodox gap year between years one and two.

Embarking on my twenties the way I did was a dream come true. I was dancing every day in the studio, teaching classes, having constant dance rehearsals for one to two shows a month. Towards the end of the year, I was offered an exciting dance role in the musical Bombay Dreams although it meant taking another gap year. I went to speak to LSE about the possibility, which they unsurprisingly denied. I was forced to choose between the two paths. I chose to complete my degree.

I graduated aged twenty-two with a 2:1 in hand, which at that time was a prerequisite for any of the high profile investment banking or management consulting jobs. I chose to pick up dance once again. The money, however, was an unreliable source to live off as I damaged my knee a few months in and was put out of commission for several weeks. I couldn't afford to not earn; I joined the corporate world at twenty-three for that stable pay cheque.

The trend continued throughout my twenties in that I was never really satisfied with spending most of my waking hours of this finite life I've been given doing what I needed to versus what I wanted to. Upon graduating with a maths degree, all of my friends were joining one of the bulge bracket banks to earn the highest starting salary available for a graduate at the time, but I wanted to travel. Marrying my need to earn with a strong desire to explore the world, I joined a graduate programme at LexisNexis – a company I had admittedly never even heard of at the time – purely because it offered a programme that allowed me to live in Germany and New York over two years while rotating across various divisions and teams.

Two years of living abroad flew by, after which I rolled off the graduate programme and settled back into the London office in a corporate strategy position. I was extremely fortunate with the opportunities I was still being given – managerial responsibilities at a young age, continued language classes, a sponsorship to study executive education at London Business School. Soon, though, without the excitement of exploring new countries and cultures, I started to feel restless.

I sat down with my first ever mentor, Tomas Romero, to get some advice on what I should be doing next. Diving straight in he asked, "What's your end goal?"

I said with conviction, "To start my own business one day!"

"Why?" he probed.

"Because I want to choose what I work on every day, how, where, when..."

Tomas looked at me sceptically and challenged, "You think running your own business is the way to achieve that?"

"Well, I certainly know it can't be achieved by working for someone else!"

Accepting my perhaps naïve rationale, he switched gears with, "Can you sell?" He was greeted with dumbstruck silence. Forget selling, even the thought of public speaking made me anxious! Tomas advised me to get some sales experience, as apparently having this skill set would be a critical component in me one day running a successful venture.

So I quit my corporate strategy role at LexisNexis and moved to a company called The Corporate Executive Board where I sold best practice research to Chief Financial Officers and Group Treasurers in the UK, Netherlands and

Denmark. After six months of being there, I became one of their top salespeople globally. A further six months on, I was promoted to head up a sales team and my geographic remit doubled.

Career progression couldn't have been better but I was still dissatisfied. Instead of basking in the cultures of the many countries I was now privileged enough to travel to, I was pit stopping at airports across continental Europe, sick to death of living out of a suitcase week in week out. Around the same time, my mother was diagnosed with cancer. It was an emotionally consuming period, and instead of getting what I believed to be entitled leeway, I began to feel like a micromanaged cash cow. Suddenly my outperformance was expected and anything short of it was put under the spotlight. Which in turn, counterproductively, meant that my day-to-day job swiftly took a back seat and I had to learn how to become a 26-year-old politician, navigating my way through the corporate drama and the gross injustice that I, melodramatically in hindsight, felt I was being subjected to at the time. Most importantly though, I had gotten what I needed from the role – I had learned how to sell. All in all, it was time to leave. But this time I did not want to jump into another job. I craved an empty work calendar so that I could reset and focus on what I was passionate about: dancing, learning languages, travelling. I needed cash flow if I wanted to give up a salary to indulge in hobbies. After all, it's far easier to reinvent oneself with a safety net!

By twenty-seven, the disciplined way in which I had

saved part of my base salary and discretionary bonuses had culminated into a £60K deposit for my first buy to let property. The day I completed the transaction, I quit my job at The Corporate Executive Board. I used my new rental income to get a flat-share in Barcelona so that I could learn Spanish every morning while going to salsa classes every evening!

A year later I enrolled at INSEAD Business School to do my MBA. INSEAD is known for producing and grooming entrepreneurs, and just like the majority of graduates from there, I finished the degree with a new business idea. Months of pitching to investors were fruitful and resulted in me securing funding for my tech startup, but it came with a caveat: I needed to demonstrate 100% faith in and commitment to the startup's commercial success by declining all job offers; as the investor eloquently put it, the basic need for an income would put "my back up against the wall" and force me to fight hard (for his money). Burdened with a €52,000 student loan, zero savings and no residential place of my own, I chose the safe route and shelved my business idea to accept the Goldman Sachs offer on the table. I rejoined the rat race.

Akin to most, the overarching theme to my twenties was that I always felt compelled to ultimately choose the more sensible path, the route to a stable income, even though I evidently spent the decade desperately trying to rebel against it. Thankfully, my first property showed me the light at the end of the tunnel. In between my job at The Corporate

Executive Board and my job at Goldman Sachs, the rent from that one flat alone allowed me to spend almost two years living the way I wanted: I lived in Spain, in France, in Singapore; I travelled the world, danced, learned different languages; and I received my MBA, something I'd always wanted to do but could never really fathom how I would afford the tuition and the living expenditures. Passive income had bought me freedom. I realised that if I could accrue a few more properties and thus increase my passive income, I could comfortably live the rest of my life this way.

By the age of thirty-five, my properties were earning me just as much as my front-office full-time job at arguably one of the world's top investment banks, and yet, I was spending two-thirds of my waking life dedicated to this corporation. Did I love the job? Yes. Were there other ways in which I wanted to spend the better part of my youth? Hell yes! I quit my job.

INTRODUCTION

THE KEYS TO FINANCIAL FREEDOM

Passive Income Is Cash Flow Received on a Regular Basis Without Actively Working

Most people will spend their teens studying, their twenties, thirties, forties and fifties working, they will finally retire somewhere in their sixties with hopefully a pension in hand that provides some cash flow, cash flow that will at long last eradicate the *need to work* every day and offer the *choice to live* every day. We hope, if not assume, that we will get to live that long, that our health will be intact when that day arrives, and that everyone we love and would want to finally spend time with will still be around and able.

The majority of us also have too much faith in job security. Let's say you're one of the lucky ones who adore their jobs and want to spend most of their lives with the people they work with; you wouldn't dream of quitting even if you won the lottery! Is it necessary for you fortunate few to have some recurring cash flow coming in from investments as well? Absolutely. What would happen to your standard of living if something health-related were to prevent you from working, or if the UK economy were to collapse and spread redundancies like wildfire, or if artificial intelligence were to wipe out your industry in this new wave of job automation and your skills become archaic? Your savings would inevitably deplete over time, but investments... investments can produce an ongoing cash flow like a salary. After all, isn't that what financial security is? A job – you can lose; savings – they will eventually run out; perpetual cash flow that doesn't require your physical presence – ergo, financial security. Shouldn't one take charge of his or her own financial security instead of relying on an employer?

Now, imagine a world where most people still spend their teens studying in order to learn, develop and grow, but they spend their twenties working *and* investing wisely to create as much of a passive income stream for themselves as they would need to afford the kind of lifestyle they want. In other words, instead of waiting until their sixties for a pension to pay out, they start building their own 'pension' that they can access much earlier in life. They could then potentially have the option to retire somewhere in their thirties or forties where the chances would be stacked in their favour with respect to health and loved ones being around. Most importantly, they could at least have a shot at spending the majority of their lives exactly how they would want to, unencumbered by the day-to-day pressures of earning a living to survive.

I retired upon turning thirty-five from my day job, and I now consciously and in full awareness choose how to spend every single day. To be very clear, when I say retired I do not mean I intend to never work again. Quite the contrary,

I cannot wait to start my own enterprise, the same end goal I had ten years ago. When I use the word retired, I use it interchangeably with financially secure. I no longer need to work for money since a passive income stream has become sufficient enough to live off. I can now embrace a fluid, more transient lifestyle. I can choose if, where, when, how and how much I want to work, without the notorious salary being a driver. I no longer need to actively work for money since my money now actively works for me.

So what goal should you set for yourself? How much passive income is enough to trade in the daily grind? Let's differentiate firstly between what I call financial security, and what I refer to as financial freedom: financial security is having a passive income large enough to cover all necessary expenditures; financial freedom is having a passive income large enough to cover your luxury expenditures on top. Everyone will have a level they need to hit in order to be financially secure, and a somewhat higher level they need to hit in order to feel financially free. My primary goal has always been to achieve financial security as I don't plan to never earn again, rather I'd love for future earnings to come from activities revolving around my passions and lifelong desires like starting my own business. Thinking of my fellow millennials, forget changing jobs, a desire to shift careers more than once has become the norm; financial security can help facilitate that. For those that want to retire early in the traditional sense, financial freedom could be a more appropriate goal.

I have managed to build a multi-million-pound property portfolio using relatively modest corporate earnings coupled with huge expenditures, e.g. putting myself through business school. By investing systematically in property, I have displaced a corporate salary income with a rental income. It is also thanks to my first two buy to lets that I was able to even save up enough of a deposit and buy a residential home.

The essence of this book is not about running a property empire. This is a book about using residential property in its simplest form, buying to rent out, and creating enough passive income that rivals what you would be making in your regular day job, thereby setting you on the path to financial freedom. I do not insist at all that property is the asset class for you, but I say with full conviction that everyone should be investing their cash in income-generating assets in order to create cash flow. Use your money to make you money!

Buy To Let Loose demystifies the buy to let process and details a very practical step-by-step guide using case studies of my first eight investments. Through my first two purchases we will explore getting a mortgage and releasing money against properties that have grown in value, and we will delve into the challenges and restrictions around doing so against certain types of properties. Using the next two case studies we will cover the essentials around what you need to look out for at property viewings, and what to expect and ask of your solicitor. My fifth property purchase will address the new tax changes that impact rental profits and list the pros and cons of setting up a limited company in an effort to preserve them, while the sixth will look at investment areas that still offer attractive returns. Property Seven underpins the success of a buy to let strategy – getting a good price – as it stipulates eight key factors that together form an effective negotiating strategy. Finally, the eighth case study will go into the preparation required before quitting that infamous day job.

I have strived to make the content conducive to less talk and more action by using concrete and current case studies that aid practical application versus penning down general concepts that form yet another theory book. To further serve that cause, I have created the Buy To Let Loose app[1] to support anyone that has begun or would like to embark on the property-investing route. The app houses six calculators that are essential tools to sanity check buy to let properties before you invest in them:

1. The **Buying Property** calculator will decipher the investments that financially make sense for you and the lender.
2. The **Stamp Duty** calculator will tell you the amount of stamp duty land tax you would owe for a buy to let purchase.
3. The **Negotiating Price** calculator will indicate the kind of offers you could make. It incorporates the eight factors discussed in Property Seven.

---

1   Available at www.buytoletloose.com, the App Store and Google Play.

4. The **Releasing Equity** calculator will evaluate how much money could be extracted from existing buy to let investments.
5. The **Mortgage Repayment** calculator will determine what your monthly repayment would be for an interest-only mortgage.
6. The **Monthly Profit** calculator will estimate the net profit you would be left with after your expenses and approximate tax liability.

I truly believe that not only can the Buy To Let Loose strategy be emulated, the results can be astronomically improved as my full appreciation for financial independence only came to fruition in my thirties; the younger you start, the faster and/or richer you will retire.

With age comes limitation. Start living sooner.

PROPERTY ONE

GETTING A MORTGAGE

A Good Mortgage Broker Is a Great Teacher

Whatever your earning capacity, it is essential to determine how much you can afford to save after sufficiently covering your basic living costs. Save as much as you realistically can and concentrate your efforts on buying income-generating assets. I promise you, to forgo some of the one-off nice-to-haves now, in return for perpetual cash flow that can sustainably buy you all the luxuries you want later, will be a sacrifice you look back on as well worth making.

The first monthly pay cheque I got at LexisNexis in May 2005 was £1,800 net. I had just read *Rich Dad Poor Dad* by Robert T. Kiyosaki on a family holiday in Portugal, & I thank my dear friend who recommended it to me as it was precisely the discipline I needed to *'pay myself first'*.[2] I set up a standing order from my current account that siphoned £600 into a savings account every month. After a year I

---

2 The book teaches the importance of always putting a portion of your earnings into income-generating assets. It argues that this should be your #1 priority and accordingly introduces the concept of 'paying yourself first' – before the taxman, your landlord, your service providers, etc.

increased it to £700, and as my salary rose with a new job in October 2007, it became £900 a month that was religiously being transferred.

By summer 2009 I had saved £60K after four years of clipping a stable pay cheque and year-end bonuses. I decided to look for my first property investment. Now, some will manage to save that in ten years and some in one, therefore the size of your first investment will depend on your individual circumstances and £60K is by no means any sort of minimum. When we come to Property Seven, you will see that I have recently invested in a property for £25K all in. So set a target and timeline that feels comfortable for you; investment opportunities are plentiful.

To refresh, that summer was the aftermath of the financial crisis and while most people were apprehensive to invest their money anywhere, some see a downturn as an opportunity:

> *"Bear markets are the biggest opportunity to build wealth because that's when everything goes on sale!"*
> – Tony Robbins, author of *Unshakeable*

So what kind of property could £60K buy me? 90% loan-to-value (LTV) mortgages were obsolete for buy to lets, i.e. if a house cost £100K, banks were previously more than willing to lend £90K if the buyer stumped up the 10% deposit of £10K. Now the maximum loan being offered to first-time buyers is 75% LTV and hence a 25% deposit was needed. Reengineering this I determined my budget. Out of £60K,

I carved out £5K for legal fees, stamp duty tax and frictional costs[3] and concluded that a £55K deposit could afford me a £220K property.

I started hunting for properties on Zoopla with a £250K maximum price set in the search filters, assuming I could negotiate a discount of at least 10%. I ascertained very quickly that one could get a lot more bang for their buck in terms of size, number of bedrooms and proximity to central London by looking at flats versus houses.

Flats Versus Houses

The fundamental reason why a flat is typically cheaper than a house is when you buy a house, you will usually be buying the freehold with it. That is, you will own the land and the house on it until you decide to sell. Flats, on the other hand, are usually sold with a leasehold interest, e.g. one hundred years. This means that the purchaser is buying the flat but technically renting the land it is on from a freeholder. At the end of the hundred-year term, the freeholder who owns the land could force you out of 'your' flat.

It is common practice for flat owners to continuously extend the leases of their flats by applying to the freeholder. The process is quite straightforward and carried out by a solicitor, although the cost of doing so can vary from a couple of thousand pounds to tens of thousands depending on the value of the property, the location, the annual ground

---

3   More detail on fees in Property Four

rent charges (how much the leaseholder pays the freeholder to rent the land), and how long is left on the lease. Crucially, if the remaining lease drops below eighty years, there is also a marriage value[4] fee that becomes payable.

To illustrate, let's say a London flat worth £250K has a remaining lease of eighty years and an annual ground rent of £10. Indicatively, a remaining lease of eighty years would probably not cost more than £5K to extend since there would be no marriage value to pay. However, if the lease lapses just one more year to seventy-nine years, the marriage value premium kicks in and the lease extension cost could double to £10K. And falling further to sixty years, the cost could easily reach a staggering £30K. Therefore, my advice is to monitor the lengths of leases on any flats you buy and to extend them once they get close to the eighty-year mark. It is important to note that if you do buy a leasehold flat, you must own it for two years before you can apply to extend the lease.

Another difference between houses and flats is blocks of flats normally come with annual service charges that the owner is responsible for. While these service charges usually pay for things like communal areas being cleaned, security for the block, lift maintenance and buildings insurance (which a house owner would ordinarily have to arrange and pay for themselves), these costs mount up over the years and are not mandatory with freeholds.

---

4   A flat with a long lease is more valuable than a flat with a short lease. If a lease is renewed, the corresponding flat rises in value. Marriage value is half that increase in value and becomes payable when the lease being renewed is less than eighty years.

Assuming I could find one with a long lease and reasonably priced service charges, I decided to go for a flat. This now left me with a choice between a private flat and an ex-local authority flat. Ex-local authority properties (also known as ex-council) were once owned by the local council and rented out to low-income households. A housing act that was enforced in the eighties under Thatcher's government, the Right to Buy scheme, allowed the tenants to buy the homes from the council at heavily discounted prices, deeming the properties ex-council. The £220K budget seemed to stretch even further with these types of flats.

Let's delve into the pitfalls of buying ex-local properties and why they are offered at a significant discount to their private property counterparts:

- Not all lenders will lend on ex-local properties, and the ones that do can sometimes have lower LTV caps. For example, a lender could lend on an ex-local flat but may cap their lending at 75% LTV whereas they could be willing to lend 80% LTV on a private flat (assuming it's not a first-time buyer).

- Lots of ex-local blocks are built from concrete as opposed to traditional brick, which again restricts the number of lenders you can access as many refuse to lend on buildings of non-standard construction.

- Many ex-local blocks are high-rise buildings and lending criteria can be quite strict when it comes to the number of stories a block has: many lenders do not lend on ex-local flats that have more than four or five stories (please note that the ground floor constitutes one storey), and the lenders that do will most likely stipulate that the block must have a lift. Lenders also get stricter on high-rise blocks the further afield they are from central London.

- Another typical trait of an ex-local block is something called deck- or balcony-access. This is when there is a continuous balcony onto which the front door of each flat on that level opens. Very few lenders accept deck-access flats, and the ones that do may not offer you the most preferential products.

- Ex-local flats are typically in blocks that have a 'council estate' vibe and can detract certain buyers/renters.

- A rather abstract criterion is how much of the ex-local block is privately owned versus still owned by the council. Many lenders will require it to be majority privately owned. I say abstract because it is hard to gauge and even the surveyor that conducts the valuation will take a judgment call. The only way to get an exact percentage is by calling the council that the block of flats falls under. [My sister is currently buying her first buy to let flat and her lender rejected the application saying that the ex-local block of flats was still majority council owned. We contacted Enfield Council, they confirmed it was 50/50, her broker relayed that to the lender and they subsequently issued a mortgage offer.]

- Ex-local flats can be subject to a section 20 (major works). On average every 5–7 years, the council whose borough the block falls under will carry out heavy duty refurbishment and maintenance like converting all windows to double-glazing, fixing the roof, redecorating, etc. The cost of works for the block would then be split among the flats resulting in a major works bill of broadly anywhere from £2K-£20K per flat (at times much more for very run down blocks). While on the plus side you would, in fact, be investing that money into your flat, you would have no control over the timing, the extent of the works, the contractors used and therefore the costs.

- Ex-local flats can also be subject to compulsory purchase orders (CPO). Typically if the area is under regeneration, the council can force you to sell the flat back to them at market value, plus you would get an additional statutory 7.5% and a negotiated 'disturbance' premium comprising all the fees associated with selling and replacing the property with a new one (e.g. legal fees, stamp duty, associated mortgage costs).

Taking all of the aforementioned into account, the flat I had my heart set on was a three-bedroom ex-local deck-access flat in Shepherd's Bush with an asking price of £240K. Westfield London shopping centre was less than a year old and around the corner, so I presumed that rental demand would be at least stable given the number of new jobs. Additional plus points were that Shepherd's Bush neighbours the affluent Holland Park, is situated in zone 2 so is very close to central London, and has accessible transport links.

I managed to negotiate a purchase price of £219K, so not quite the 10% discount I was aiming for, but considering three-bedroom flats in the area were renting for £2K per calendar month (pcm) at the time, it was too good a gross[5] yield to let go of:

GROSS YIELD

$$\frac{\text{Annual Rent}}{\text{Purchase Price}} = \text{Gross Yield (\%)}$$

£24,000 / £219,000 = 11%

Gross yield is a crude and indicative measure since it does not accurately tell you how much net profit you will pocket, and it does not take into account any refurbishment costs

---

5   Before mortgage repayments, service charges, maintenance and any tax due.

required on top of the purchase price. It should instead be used as a quick calculation to identify attractive opportunities. For example, an investment offering a gross yield of 5%+ when interest rates on cash in the bank are virtually zero is worth looking into. I decided to set my hurdle rate at 10%, which means the minimum return I desired in order to make a property investment worthwhile for me was 10%.[6]

I strongly advise you to set a hurdle rate of your own as it is crucial to not only separate the wheat from the chaff, but it also helps you to compare investment opportunities when multiple options are on the table. Setting a hurdle rate helps you to make decisions rationally as well instead of being driven emotionally, especially with the first couple of purchases where one can be particularly sensitive to how much they are spending in absolute terms! I learned this the hard way...

About six months prior, I had mentioned to a family friend that I was interested in buy to let opportunities. He had told me about a one-bedroom flat in north-west London being sold for £125K. I hadn't really done my homework at that point but was so keen to get started, I sent my dad and sister (an architect and an interior & spatial designer) to the open day to go and view the property. They confirmed it 'looked good' and subsequently offered full asking price at my request and on my behalf. The flat was taken off the

---

6   Hurdle rate is also known as weighted average cost of capital (WACC), required rate of return and target rate.

market and the legal proceedings commenced. I was an eager beaver, wet behind the ears – I hadn't even seen the property, hadn't tried to negotiate, I was just too consumed with excitement at the thought of becoming a property owner. A few weeks into the legal proceedings, my solicitor mentioned in passing over the phone that the flat had been bought by the current owner a couple of months earlier in an auction for £95K. I remember feeling so duped at the time, that someone was making £30K in a few weeks thanks to my naivety and impatience to invest. I pulled out of the deal. The owner even dropped the price to £120K but I refused and didn't want to pay a penny over £100K! Needless to say, the deal fell through. In hindsight, I acted irrationally. The £13K annual rent I would have gotten at the time would have still given me a 10% yield, but I begrudged a random person getting a phenomenal deal and therefore lost out on a great deal. Nose, spite, face? That flat would have been worth £250K today. So for anyone like me that wants to feel they are always getting the best deal, set yourself a hurdle rate and adhere to it because more often than not you will be lining someone else's pockets by buying the property for more than they did. Why? Nobody wants to sell at a loss unless they are forced to by circumstance.

Specifically with property, hurdle rates also help you to set your maximum budget. Back to the live Shepherd's Bush example, in order to maintain my minimum 10% desired return, assuming the rent I could obtain was £2K a month, the maximum purchase price I could offer was £240K:

MAXIMUM PURCHASE PRICE

$$\frac{\text{Annual Rent}}{\text{Hurdle Rate (\%)}} = \text{Maximum Purchase Price}$$

£24,000 / 10% = £240,000

Paying anything more would have reduced my gross yield to sub 10%, e.g. had I paid £245K, the gross yield would have been £24,000 / £245,000 = 9.8%.[7]

Setting a hurdle rate also sets the minimum rent you should charge:

MINIMUM RENT REQUIRED

Purchase Price x Hurdle Rate (%) = Minimum Annual Rent

£219,000 x 10% = £21,900

In order to maintain my 10% return I needed to charge £21,900 a year in rent, that is £1,825 pcm.

So as you can see, having your own hurdle rate immediately sets parameters in place for you. Investment

---

7   These calculations are incorporated into the Negotiating Price calculator on the Buy To Let Loose app.

opportunities are endless and parameters help to fairly, by removing any emotional bias, identify which opportunities are viable and which are not. They allow you to focus your energy and attention and they form the basis of an efficient buy to let process.

The real obstacle now was to secure a mortgage, especially given the pitfalls discussed when it comes to finding a lender for an ex-local property. Two of the prominent mortgage brokers in London back then were Alexander Hall and John Charcol. These two outfits charged a fee to use them, however, they could also access most of the lenders out there. Mortgage brokers do get retrocession fees[8] from the lenders as well and as a result, most freelance brokers can afford to not charge you at all. To save the extra money, I went for a freelance broker that a friend recommended.

The broker applied to a prominent high street lender for me and after one month, he came back and said my mortgage had been rejected without reason! I went straight to John Charcol who appointed me a mortgage broker. I paid £500 in fees and within two weeks had a mortgage offer. It was worth every penny. The John Charcol broker explained to me that there were only two lenders available at the time that would consider ex-local flats with deck-access, and the high street lender that had rejected my application wasn't one of them. How did my freelance broker not know that? Fortunately at the time, free valuations were trending so

---

8   Kick-backs or commission

I didn't lose any money, but that was down to luck rather than the savvy of this freelancer. Bear in mind that every time you apply for any type of loan, it leaves a footprint on your credit history and so unsuccessful applications can be a pain in the neck in more ways than one. I decided from then on that I would always use a professional outfit to procure mortgages for me, despite the additional cost.

There are many mortgage products on the market and it will be your broker's job to decipher the options and help you choose the optimal product to apply for. I outline below the main factors to deliberate.

Loan-to-value (LTV)

As a first-time buyer for buy to let properties, 75% LTV is typically the maximum LTV you will be able to obtain meaning a 25% deposit will be required. And so the question becomes, should you go for a lower LTV product and put down a larger deposit if you can afford it? Larger deposits mean smaller interest repayments since a) you would be borrowing less money, and b) the larger the deposit, the lower the interest rate. I wanted to put down as little as possible for the deposit (so that I could prematurely start saving for my next investment) while ensuring the deposit was significant enough to procure me a good interest rate and manageable monthly repayments. I chose a 75% LTV product where I had to put down a £54,750 deposit (25% of the £219K purchase price) and the lender would loan me the remaining £164,250 at 3.5% interest:

MONTHLY MORTGAGE REPAYMENT

$$\frac{\text{Loan Amount}}{12} \times \text{Interest Rate (\%)} = \text{Mortgage Repayment}$$

$$(\pounds164{,}250 \,/\, 12) \times 3.5\% = \pounds479.06$$

Taking out this product resulted in monthly repayments of £479.06.[9] With market rents for three-bedroom ex-local flats in Shepherd's Bush at £2K pcm, I felt more than comfortable with these repayments.

Capital repayment or interest-only
There are two ways to repay a loan:

- Capital repayment means every month you pay the interest and some of the actual loan amount off, and by the end of the mortgage term you have paid off the full loan in its entirety.

- Interest-only means you only pay the interest amount every month and at the end of the mortgage term, you still owe the full loan amount to the lender. In order to settle the balance at the end of the term, you would most likely sell the property.

---

9   These calculations apply to interest-only mortgages and are inbuilt into the Mortgage Repayment calculator on the Buy To Let Loose app.

I opted for interest-only since my aim was to maximise the monthly profit and save up that much faster for my next deposit. Furthermore, interest-only deals will characteristically have initial periods where you won't be able to repay the capital (without incurring a penalty), but thereafter you can pay off the capital in portions to reduce the loan amount. This way you get the additional cash flow to ideally save up for another deposit, but you always have the option to pay off the loan without being tied into a rigid repayment schedule. A rationale for capital repayment could be if you live in the property and want to eventually own it outright.

Mortgage term

The mortgage term defines how many years it will take you to either 100% own the property, for capital repayment mortgages, or how many years you will have until you are due to pay back the entire loan amount, for interest-only mortgages. Since I went for interest-only, I also went for the longest mortgage term available which was twenty-five years because I want to hold on to the income-generating investment for as long as possible. The rationale for choosing a shorter mortgage term would be if you are making capital repayments and would like to outright own the home in a few years.

Fixed or variable interest

The product I chose was a 3% variable interest rate above the Bank of England (BoE) base rate for two years, which then reverted to 4.2%. That means my loan was subject to an interest rate of 3% + the BoE base rate of 0.5% at the time which equals 3.5%. The variable aspect means my rate was subject to change as and when the base rate changed during those two years, so if the base rate reduced to 0%, my overall interest rate would have become 3% and the monthly repayments would have reduced, and similarly had the base rate increased to 1%, my overall interest rate would have become 4% and the monthly repayments would have increased.

Conversely, a fixed rate implies just that, that no matter what happens to the base rate or anything else in the economy, your interest rate is fixed for the number of years stipulated. To have that certainty you would usually be charged a slightly higher interest and so in this case, I had the option of fixing the rate at 4% for two years. Now the base rate is linked directly to the health of the UK economy: simplistically, at times of prosperity, the UK government can afford to increase interest rates (to combat inflation), and during poor growth periods, the government can suppress interest rates in an effort to boost the economy. Seeing as we were still very much in a fragile state post the financial crisis, I took a call that interest rates were not going to rise any time soon and chose the variable interest rate product.

The reversion rate of 4.2% refers to what one pays once the two years are over, but typically you'd remortgage the product before the rate reverts. We will introduce and explore remortgaging in Property Two.

Mortgage fees

In addition to the mortgage broker fee, many mortgage products have a valuation fee, an arrangement fee, and some charge an additional processing or application fee. The valuation fee will be a function of the value of the property where lenders have a fee schedule. All lenders will require you to undertake a basic mortgage valuation and sometimes the lender will absorb the cost for you. There is usually an option to upgrade the kind of report you commission as well: a HomeBuyer report costs a couple of hundred pounds more and brings your attention to some of the possible structural issues like damp or subsidence; a full structural survey costs a few hundred pounds more and proves very useful for older properties where detailed advice is included around the major refurbishment required. Whichever option you choose, the valuation fee needs to be paid upfront. Similarly, any processing fees will be standard and required upfront. Arrangement fees, on the other hand, can either be paid upfront or added to the loan amount.

The product I opted for offered a free basic valuation and had no additional processing fees, but it did come with a £995 arrangement fee that I chose to add to the loan. Consequently, my full loan amount increased to £165,245 and my monthly repayments increased by £2.90 to £481.96. To pay an extra £2.90 a month for two years versus an upfront payment of £995 was well worth it to me seeing as I was trying to minimise my cash outlay and save up already for my second property investment. Why? Because the prospect of making a 10% return on another investment was far more enticing than holding cash in the bank earning 0.5%.

Lending Criteria

Having a good mortgage broker is like having your own personal property consultant – ask lots of questions to understand the process, the lenders out there, and their respective lending criteria. It will all become invaluable when hunting for good property investments. Even if you plan to purchase a property with cash and will never require a mortgage, you may want to sell it one day to someone that does and therefore, it is beneficial to understand what aspects of a property are lender unfriendly.

I outline some general guidelines on what lenders dislike:

- High rise blocks (> 4 stories)
- Non-standard construction (concrete, timber – anything that isn't made from brick)
- Flat roof as opposed to a pitched roof
- Deck-access (ex-local specific)
- Remaining lease < 70 years
- Freehold flats
- Very run down or no kitchen/bathroom
- Structural issues like a missing ceiling or a damaged roof
- Excessive damp

- Subsidence and remedial underpinning without a 10-year warranty
- Japanese knotweed within proximity (a plant that damages buildings)
- Properties above commercial premises (a restaurant, shops, offices, etc.)
- Majority still council owned (ex-local specific)
- Borrower with a base salary < £25K
- Poor credit rating

All of the above, bar the last three restrictions, can be seen directly when viewing the property or referred to the estate agent who should be able to clarify.

The antepenultimate restriction around the majority of a block still being council owned can either be verified by the council as mentioned earlier (although they can take some time to come back to you), or a simple way of getting a rough idea is to check sold prices on Zoopla: enter the postcode of the flat in question in the 'house prices' section of the website and tally up the sales in that block to gauge how many the council have sold. The reason this is a crude measure is that not all sales are always posted and you could be underestimating how much of the block is actually privately owned.

With respect to the penultimate restriction around the base salary, £25K+ is a requirement for most lenders (but not all), so it's worth keeping this in mind when negotiating your pay! For those of you who are self-employed, we will discuss earnings required when we come to Property Eight.

The last restriction around having a poor credit rating will affect your ability to borrow money for any investment, period. You will either be denied a mortgage or you will only be able to access mortgages with uncompetitive to extortionate interest rates. Most people do not think about their credit rating until it is time to apply for a mortgage. Do not do this! Keeping your credit rating in check is imperative to borrowing money, otherwise known as leverage, and leverage is a key tool for scaling investments. Without a mortgage, envisage how long it would take you to save £219K cash, and if you are fortunate enough to say "not long", could you not consider using all of that cash to buy four properties as opposed to one?

There are three leading credit agencies in the UK: Equifax, Experian and Callcredit. You can check your credit scores with each agency and they will broadly mirror one other, although you can get slight variations due to lag times of things being reflected. The reason it is important to ensure all three reports are in good health is that lenders use different agencies to conduct their credit checks and sometimes a combination of two.

Here are some of the things that are detrimental to your credit score:

- Not being on the electoral roll
- No credit history – sounds counterintuitive but if you have no debts, how can they judge the likelihood of you making timely repayments?

- High or maximum credit utilisation, meaning if you are able to borrow a maximum of £5K on your credit card and you are always close to or at that limit
- County court judgments (CCJ), when the court formally recognises that you owe a party money after several attempts to retrieve it from you – CCJs stay on your credit report for six years
- Too many credit requests in a short period of time

If you get rejected for a mortgage due to your credit rating, find out from your broker the specific credit agency the lender used, get a copy of your report and go through it with your broker to spruce it up in whichever way you can. For instance, if you have recently moved home and your registration on the electoral roll has not been reflected in your report, call up the council, get a letter of confirmation from them that you are indeed on the roll, forward it to the credit agency and chase them to have it reflected. You could also check all three reports and if one scores above the rest, you could be selective with the lenders you apply to; a good mortgage broker will know which lenders refer checks to which credit agencies.

Fortunately I managed to secure a mortgage and all in all, the transaction ran quite smoothly and swiftly. I got the keys to my first buy to let investment in October 2009 and spent circa £2K getting the flat prepared for rental:

- A fresh lick of paint
- Some basic furniture (bed, sofa, dining table & chairs)
- Carpets
- Curtains
- Gas safety certificate (to confirm the boiler is safe)
- Electrics safety certificate (to confirm the wiring is safe)
- White goods (fridge, freezer)

Summing up the 25% deposit, stamp duty, advisor fees and refurbishment costs, my full cash outlay was £62K. I procured tenants by November and negotiated £1,907 pcm, £82 more than the minimum rent I had set myself. After deducting the mortgage repayment, the service charges and the ground rent from the rental income, I was making an incremental £1,300 profit a month. A way to quantify this is by using the following formula that evaluates how much you are earning on your cash invested:

RETURN ON INVESTMENT (ROI)

$$\frac{\text{Annual Profit}}{\text{Cash Invested}} = \text{Return On Investment (\%)}$$

$$(\pounds1,300 \times 12) / \pounds62,000 = 25.2\%$$

This 25.2% is the annual return on the cash invested and can be directly compared to the 0.5% per annum I would have been earning in the bank had I left the cash uninvested.

Another useful measure to look at is the estimated payback period. That is, how many years it will take to earn back the amount invested:

PAYBACK PERIOD

$$\frac{\text{Cash Invested}}{\text{Annual Profit}} = \text{Payback Period (years)}$$

£62,000 / (£1,300 x 12) = 3.97 years

This means it would take my investment four years to earn back the £62K, and thereafter any profit made could effectively feel like it's coming from a free investment! In other words, once you've gotten your investment money paid back and have none of your cash left invested, we could say that the return on investment (ROI) increases to infinity (∞) since you'd effectively have zero money still making you money:[10]

$$(£1,300 \times 12) / £0 = \infty$$

For those of you unexcited by maths where the word infinity screams snooze fest (!), let's break it down year by year:

---

10   Mathematically, any number divided by zero is infinity.

Year 0

We begin with me putting £62,000 savings into a property investment. That £62,000 will earn a monthly profit of £1,300 equating to an annual profit of £15,600.

$$ROI = £15,600 / £62,000 = 25.2\%$$

Year 1

After a year I have made £15,600 in profit. I was £62,000 out of pocket, now I'm £46,400 out of pocket. In other words, my remaining invested cash is £46,400, still making an annual profit of £15,600.

$$ROI = £15,600 / £46,400 = 33.6\%$$

Year 2

Another year later, another £15,600 in profit... now I've gotten more than half my money back and have a remaining investment of £30,800, still earning the same annual profit.

$$ROI = £15,600 / £30,800 = 50.6\%$$

Year 3

Banking another £15,600 in profit, I now only have £15,200 left in the investment. That £15,200 cash will still earn £15,600 profit a year. My remaining investment is doubling itself now.

$$ROI = £15,600 / £15,200 = 102.6\%$$

Year 4

Four years later, cashing in another £15,600 profit means I have now taken back my full £62,000 investment. I have broken even. And the £0 remaining investment is STILL earning me £15,600 profit.

$$\text{ROI} = £15,600 / 0 = \infty$$

Without a single penny of my cash left in the investment, I continue to benefit from continuous income. That is what an ROI of infinity means.

Let's summarise the investment:

Property One	
Purchase price	£219,000
Monthly rent	£1,907
	$\Rightarrow$ Gross yield 10%
Return On Investment	
Cash investment	£62,000
Annual profit[11]	£15,600
	$\Rightarrow$ ROI in 2009 was 25%
Payback Period	
Estimated payback period	4 years
Actual payback period	3 years
Equity released to date	£85,000
Remaining investment	£0
	$\Rightarrow$ ROI since 2012 is ∞

11   Net of mortgage repayments, service charges and ground rent

It is important to highlight here that the estimated payback period should always be used as a crude measure to compare investments as the actual payback period will always differ: releasing equity from your investment will give you cash back at a quicker rate and reduce the actual payback period; unexpected maintenance costs will keep your money invested for longer and increase the payback period; changes in interest rates will affect the annual profit and therefore the rate at which you get your investment back.

I should also emphasise that 'remaining investment' refers to how much of my initial cash outlay remains in the property. This is different to the equity I still hold in the property, which today is 35% of the current market value as I'm on a 65% LTV product. In other words, if I sold the property for full market value, I would pay back 65% of the sale proceeds to the lender and 35% of the sale proceeds would belong to me.[12]

And so in actuality, I got the full £62K cash investment back after just three years, I continue to hold an income-generating asset that feeds me rental profits every month despite having no cash left invested in the property, and I still own a 35% equity stake in the flat!

Without investing in this property, £62K savings at the bank would have earned me approximately £300 a year. Instead, that £62K has produced over £15K profit a year.

---

12   My portion of the sale proceeds would be subject to transaction fees and capital gains tax.

Furthermore, over time I have been able to release £85K cash from the property to fund future purchases. We will examine how to do this in Property Two.

To conclude, let's pull out the key takeaways from this chapter:

✓ SAVE A FIXED AMOUNT OF SALARY EVERY MONTH
✓ ASSUME A 25% DEPOSIT & DETERMINE YOUR BUDGET
✓ SET YOUR OWN HURDLE RATE
✓ ELIMINATE UNMORTGAGEABLE PROPERTIES
✓ USE A BROKER THAT CAN ACCESS MOST LENDERS
✓ KEEP YOUR CREDIT RATING IN CHECK

PROPERTY TWO

THE POWER OF LEVERAGE

One Way to Scale a Portfolio Quickly Is to Borrow Wisely

I graduated from INSEAD in July 2011, at which point I held no savings having spent shy of the last two years without a job. I still had the £1,300 monthly profit coming in, although I hadn't been able to save a penny of this as making the most of business school student life clearly came at a cost! Moreover, I now had a €52,000 student loan to service. I thus parked the tech startup idea I had worked so passionately on to instead commence a paid internship at Goldman Sachs.

I managed to save most of the internship pay as I continued to live off the £1,300 monthly rental income, but soon to kick in was my new cash outflow of student loan repayments at £700 a month. I was fortunate enough to receive a full-time offer from Goldman Sachs but the job didn't start until January 2012. I could have dipped into the savings I now had, but sticking to the ethos I was cultivating, my income (regular cash flow) was for spending and the capital (savings) was for investing. Luckily, my initial two-year period on the Shepherd's Bush flat was coming to an end.

To refresh, why is it important to remortgage at the end of the initial period? If you recall, had I let the product continue, at the end of the two years the interest rate would have increased to the bank's reversion rate of 4.2%. And so it is imperative to browse products on the market and switch if necessary to ensure your rate remains competitive. The key thing needed to access the right products is the updated value of the property. As mentioned in Property One, a lower LTV product commands a lower interest rate. For instance, my 75% LTV mortgage against the Shepherd's Bush flat had charged me 3% over base, however, had I chosen a 65% LTV product, not only would my loan amount have been less, the rate I would have been charged would have been less, supposedly 2.5% over base. If you can now show the lender that the actual loan relative to the property value is less than the initial LTV you had, you will get access to cheaper products. We shall see this with my example below.

I went onto Zoopla to gauge how much an ex-local three-bedroom flat in Shepherd's Bush then cost. Asking prices averaged £230K-£250K. I had hoped there would have been a more significant increase in property values in those two years, especially given I had bought right after the financial crisis when property valuations were suppressed. But as some of you may recall, 2011/12 was for a short while considered a double-dip recessionary period. It was later verified that the UK did not undergo two consecutive quarters of negative GDP growth, thereby deeming the double-dip recession invalid, but as with all markets the mere perception is very influential.

I had my lender undertake a valuation of the flat and it came back at £238,500. Therefore, with an outstanding mortgage balance of £165,245, I had two options:

1. I could reduce the LTV of my loan from 75% to 70%, since the amount the bank was lending me was now only 70% of the current value (£165,245 / £238,500 = 69.3%). By switching to a product from the 70% LTV category, I could access a lower interest rate.
2. I could stay within the 75% LTV category and keep my borrowing to that ratio. 75% of the new valuation was £178,875 meaning I could borrow up to that much. Subtracting the outstanding mortgage balance at that point of £165,245, I could still borrow a further £13,630.

I chose the second option. By releasing £13,630 and adding it to my internship savings meant I was getting notably closer to that second deposit. Yes I would have to pay more interest as the mortgage amount would increase, and yes I would have to pay it off at a higher rate if sticking to the 75% LTV category as opposed to 70%, but essentially what I was stating through my approach is: I can invest at a higher return than at which I can borrow. The first property investment established that I could earn 25% return on my cash investment. I welcomed the opportunity to pay 3–4% interest on that £13K for a prospective 25% payout on that same £13K. The equity release would meaning-fully accelerate reaching the deposit required for a second property purchase, another income-generating asset that would work towards getting me to my end goal, financial security.

Separately, I needed some of the equity release to cover my student loan repayments until I started earning again – another reminder that my passive income was not yet enough to live off and that I still needed to actively work.

When remortgaging you can either simply switch to a new product with the incumbent lender, or you can transfer your mortgage to another lender if you feel their products are more suitable, although in this case a solicitor would be required and legal fees would apply. For that reason, when weighing up products on the market, the cost incurred to switch lenders needs to be taken into account. If you do switch to a new lender, you will also have to go through all the same checks you went through at the purchase stage: credit checks, income proof, property valuation, etc. Additionally, they will want to see your tenancy agreement to ensure it meets their lending criteria. Most lenders require assured shorthold tenancy (AST) agreements, essentially twelve months or less, and many lenders do not like properties being let to council tenants or to private companies. In short, there should be a good reason to switch lenders given the additional cost, time and effort involved.

With my flat being ex-local, deck-access and a five-storey

building, the lenders available to me were limited. I chose to stay with the same one and identified all of the 75% LTV products available to me. I opted once again for a variable product that offered a slightly lower rate than its fixed interest counterpart, as even though the UK did not suffer from another recession, it was still far off from prosperity; an interest rate hike in the subsequent two years seemed unlikely. I chose a two-year product, 3.4% + base so totalling an overall rate of 3.9%, again tagged with a £995 arrangement fee. My new loan amount was £165,245 + £13,630 + £995 = £179,870. The £13K equity release was seamless and hit my account in October, at which point the new monthly repayments of £584.58 also began.[13]

It goes without saying, before releasing equity it is vital to ensure one feels comfortable with the increase in monthly repayments it brings: a balance is required between releasing equity and maintaining cash flow. At the same time, one shouldn't feel nervous about the *nominal* amount of debt, rather it's the *relative* amount of debt that needs to be kept at bay. For example, if you had £1m of mortgage debt across your properties and the total value of those properties was £1.1m, you would have 91% debt and 9% equity. According to most, you'd be over-leveraged. If property values were to drop and the market value of your portfolio fell to £900K, you would have negative equity since you would owe more than you own. If you had to

---

13   This calculation applies to interest-only mortgages and is inbuilt into the Mortgage Repayment calculator on the Buy To Let Loose app.

liquidate for any reason (sell the portfolio), you would get £900K in sale proceeds but would still owe £1m to your lenders. Conversely, the same £1m of debt against a property portfolio worth £2m is far better protected; property values would have to drop by half before you'd encroach negative equity.

Less the new mortgage repayment and the monthly fixed costs (service charges and ground rent), my monthly profit dropped to £1,200. Thank goodness I had taken the Goldman Sachs job and the stable monthly pay cheque that came with it, otherwise post paying off my student loan, I would have been left with £500 a month to live and feed off. This reality lit a fire under me to immediately invest in another income-generating asset, my second property.

Goldman Sachs was committed to helping the MBA students pay off part of their student loans and gave us sign-on bonuses upon commencing the role. Now, every other MBA hire used this money to reduce their student loans, thereby easing the pressure. This seemed like the sensible thing to do, especially when looking specifically at the student loan I had signed up to where I was paying a whopping 6% interest to a private company, extortion given the interest rate levels at that time. However, I felt confident that I could earn a return greater than 6% on the capital and therefore it made sense to keep borrowing the student loan money. And so taking the internship money, the equity release, and now adding the sign-on money to my 'deposit and counting', I had £45K. Reengineering that and carving out £5K once again for fees, I had £40K for a 25% deposit and a target purchase price of £160K.

I wanted to go for something that was easily accessible to central London that would guarantee a strong rental demand. I again restricted my search to flats and not houses. Sticking with my 10% hurdle rate, I calculated the minimum rent I would require:

MINIMUM RENT REQUIRED

Purchase Price x Hurdle Rate (%) = Minimum Annual Rent

£160,000 x 10% = £16,000

This equated to £1,334 pcm. I set my search filter to a maximum purchase price of £190K and identified flats that would rent out in that region. Unlike my first property where the third viewing was a charm, I must have seen at least fifteen different flats this time around and put offers on ten of them, all to be rejected. I then found a two-bed flat in a private block in Harlesden with an asking price of £190K.

I noticed it had been on the market for a few months and approached the estate agent to get some insight into the seller. He was desperate to sell. I also researched sold prices in the area and saw that the next-door flat had sold for £180K in 2010. That was before the economy had dipped again, that flat had come with a garage and this one did not, and the final negotiating tactic I had on my side was the poor condition of this flat. It was all cosmetic but nonetheless, I couldn't imagine it appealing to first-time buyers or those that were looking for a place to move in to, and I now understood the seller did not have the means to even superficially beautify it for marketing purposes. I tried my luck with a £160K offer and a promise for it to go through very quickly, and my offer was accepted!

I called up Alexander Hall this time to try a different mortgage broker. Their fee structure was different and charged 0.5% of the loan amount required. I needed a loan of £120K (75% of £160K) resulting in a £600 fee. Buying this flat allowed me access to many more products since it wasn't ex-local. I opted for the following:

- 75% LTV
- Interest-only
- 3.75% variable over base for two years
- 25-year mortgage term
- £300 valuation fee
- No arrangement or application fee

The base rate was still 0.5% in 2012 meaning my overall interest rate was 4.25%. With a loan of £120K, my monthly repayments were £425 pcm. I completed on the flat and procured tenants by the summer where I was receiving £1,350 pcm. After deducting the mortgage repayment, the service charges and the ground rent from the rental income, I was making an incremental £800 profit a month.

Aside from the 25% deposit and the £5K spent on legal fees, stamp duty and mortgage fees, I again spent circa £2K getting the flat prepared for rental. This took the full upfront cash outlay to £47K.

Let's summarise the investment:

Property Two	
Purchase price	£160,000
Monthly rent	£1,350
	⇒ Gross yield 10%
Return On Investment	
Cash investment	£47,000
Annual profit	£9,600
	⇒ ROI in 2012 was 20%
Payback Period	
Estimated payback period	5 years
Actual payback period	2 years
Equity released to date	£70,000
Remaining investment	£0
	⇒ ROI since 2014 is ∞

Without releasing £13K from the first property, it would have taken me another six months at least to buy this second property. Instead in those six months, I profited almost £5K, thanks to the power of leverage. Exercise this tool though with full caution as there's a fine line between friend and foe; leverage can also be your worst enemy. It's about maintaining a balance and only releasing equity if any increase in repayments can be comfortably managed. [If you default on the mortgage repayments, the property can get repossessed and you would lose all of your equity in the property.]

My cash outlay of £47K has been producing approximately £10K profit a year instead of sitting in my current account accruing approximately £200 a year. Also, in the same way that I released £13K from the Shepherd's Bush flat, I have since been able to release £70K cash from this Harlesden property as the flat today is worth over £300K.

Unless you have a very highly paid job and are able to save sizable deposits quickly, releasing equity in this way becomes integral to growing a property portfolio. One could also sell a property that has risen in value, but then you would lose out on future rental gains and capital gains tax would be due on the sale proceeds. I personally would only consider selling a buy to let property (before the mortgage term is up) if it were no longer profitable and the passive income play had become redundant. Otherwise in order to exploit rising property values, I always opt for releasing equity, again assuming I can manage the increase in repayments.

Now, the only way you can release equity is if the values of your properties are indeed rising. As we know, markets can go up and down so instead of banking on a rising property market, it is fundamentally important to purchase properties at a discount. **The profit is in the buying**. That way, if the property market remains stagnant or even drops slightly, the market value of your property will still likely remain higher than your purchase price. What should you be looking for in a property that adds value, and equally what aspects end up detracting value? We will tackle these in Property Three.

To conclude, let's pull out the key takeaways from this chapter:

✓ SAVE AS MUCH RENTAL INCOME AS YOU CAN
✓ REMORTGAGE TO KEEP RATES COMPETITIVE
✓ SWITCHING LENDERS INCURS LEGAL COSTS
✓ IF VALUES RISE, REDUCE LTV FOR BETTER RATES ...
✓ ... OR, CONSIDER RELEASING EQUITY TO REINVEST

PROPERTY THREE

WHAT TO LOOK FOR ON VIEWINGS

Akin to Diamonds, Know the Four Cs Before You Buy: Costs, Constraints, Chain, Charges

Three years post buying the Harlesden flat, I was still working at Goldman and earning an active income that I handled just as diligently as I did my first salary. After covering off living expenses including the student loan repayments, in three years I had accrued £50K in savings. Moreover in the same three years, I had set aside all of the additional rental income that had culminated into another £60K potential deposit. Most significantly, because the property values in the areas had increased significantly, I had managed to release a further £72K from the Shepherd's Bush flat and £70K from the Harlesden flat.

All of a sudden, I had £250K of capital to invest. How did that happen? £50K of that, yes I had saved fair and square from working an extremely demanding full-time job. But the extra £200K? It genuinely felt undeserved because I know just how much I had to scrimp and save to bank that £50K. Even if I had cut out every penny of non-essential spending and doubled the pace of saving my corporate income, it still would have taken a good few years to reach that quantum of cash.

The two buy to let properties took me from zero to sixty in the blink of an eye and jump-started my property portfolio.

I decided to use the £60K of rental income I had accumulated to buy another investment property, and to earmark the residual £190K for a residential home. In this chapter we will focus on the third buy to let property, and the residential will follow in Property Four.

Now by law of nature, it couldn't work in my favour both ways. Property values had increased significantly, hence I was able to release over £140K of equity. But increasing property values made it that much more difficult to identify buy to let investments that met my 10% hurdle rate. To demonstrate, let's recall the Harlesden property. It was still earning £1,350 a month in rent but the value of the property was now £302K. If I were to have made that same investment in 2015, it would have been at a gross yield of 5.4%:

GROSS YIELD

$$\frac{\text{Annual Rent}}{\text{Purchase Price}} = \text{Gross Yield (\%)}$$

(£1,350 x 12) / £302,000 = 5.4%

In fact, I was finding it impossible to source anything markedly better than this. London prices had risen so spectacularly, while the rental market, though still buoyant, had not comparatively risen at all. I decided to reduce my hurdle rate to 7%, meaning if I could find properties that delivered a 7% yield, it was still worth my while to invest.

To identify 7% yielding investments anywhere, let alone restricting ourselves to just property, was difficult... but not impossible. I started to look a little out of London and found that commuter hubs, in particular, offered higher yields. However, I still felt that when it came to capital appreciation and therefore being able to release equity, which was an integral component of my growth strategy, London was a safer bet. Also taking into account that I was holding down a full-time job that demanded all of my attention, I didn't have the capacity to explore areas I wasn't familiar with, even within London. In order to stick to north & west London and meet the 7% hurdle rate, I needed to find a way where I could either get a significant discount on the property purchase price and/or I could charge more rent.

Auctions

The immediate answer to getting a discounted property was procuring one through auction. I attended a few and temporarily got very excited when looking at guide prices that were 20% cheaper than market values. But for me, auctions turned out to be a little too risky.

The first auction I went to was in 2011. I specifically went because there had been a two-bedroom flat for sale in Shepherd's Bush in the same block as mine, and I was itching to see it sell for more than I had paid for my three-bed, clearly seeking some sort of validation of my investment skills. The two-bed went for £150K. It implied a three-bed wouldn't even be worth £200K, forget more than the £219K I had paid. I didn't sleep for a week!

I got over it later that year when my three-bed revalued at shy of £240K. It also gave me this unfounded confidence in auctions that if someone else could get pick up such a fantastic deal there, why couldn't I? It was 2015 now, I was four years wiser and I had found an amazing house in Acton for sale at a Barnard Marcus auction with a guide price of £220K. I set myself a budget of £250K and on a lunch break went alone and took a front row seat in this grand hall. The bidding war was between two others and me: 220 (me), 230, 240, 250 (me), 260, 270, 280 (me!), 300, 320, 340 (me!!)... I had completely lost the plot! Until that moment, I had never prayed so hard for someone to beat me at something. I couldn't afford £340K what on earth was I playing at! The adrenaline, the competitive nature the bidding pulls out of someone like me. Thankfully the property surpassed my bid and ended up going for £540K; not sure if there was gold in the back garden that I wasn't aware of but, I had never been so happy to be back at my open plan desk eating a Big Mac and watching the rain fall against my window pane.

Firstly, the good yielding properties usually get bid on quite a bit and end up getting bought at market value prices anyway, unless you try and negotiate with the corresponding auction house to seal the deal before the property officially goes on sale. Secondly, sellers put their properties through auction because they typically want a quick sale. Sometimes that could be down to a pure liquidity requirement and nothing as such is wrong with the property. But more often than not, there are unforeseen issues with auctioned properties that the buyer may only come to know of post the sale, especially if one is not allowed to see the property before, e.g. structural issues, sitting tenants or squatters, severe damp, a marketed two-bedroom flat that is in fact a purpose-built one-bedroom flat with a partition wall down the middle (which happened to me although fortunately my lawyer found that out before I bid). Now, naturally your solicitor can do some preliminary checks on the property but then you are incurring legal fees before you have even successfully outbid everyone. Thirdly, once you agree to the sale of the property, you are legally bound; you are responsible for all associated costs on the property once that hammer goes down. Thereafter if you change your mind, you would lose the 10% deposit you would have probably paid to secure the deal. Finally, you would only have twenty-eight days to complete,[14] and if for any reason your solicitor could not complete in time or if your mortgage offer took longer to come through, you would be in breach of contract and would have to either complete with cash, forfeit your deposit, and/or you could be charged interest for every day that lapses past the

---

14 This is the most common timescale although you would need to check the special conditions of each sale as that overrides standard protocol.

completion deadline. You could also be sued for any loss suffered by the seller should the property be subsequently sold for a lesser amount.

The only way I could get even close to comfortable was if I were to start the mortgage process before the auction to ensure I would get the offer in time, and I could commission a structural survey on the property. Although I knew that as soon as I started incurring costs, I would form attachments to properties and again risk overbidding in the moment. Therefore, and due to the aforementioned risks, I went back to surfing Zoopla.

Exercising patience and tenacity, I did manage to find three options online that looked promising. They all met my adjusted 7% hurdle rate, they were situated in north-west London, they were ex-local flats without deck-access so plenty of lenders would view them as suitable securities to lend against, and they all had long leases. But upon delving deeper, there was something 'wrong' with each of them:

1. One was in an ex-local block of flats where the ground floor was an office (the agent did not tell me that and you couldn't tell from the marketing pictures), which meant the property was ex-local and above commercial premises – very difficult to get a mortgage on.
2. One had a major works bill served on it (section 20) that was estimated at £20K – no wonder the seller was eager to rid the property at a reasonable price.

3. One of them had a covenant in the lease that barred the property from being let! Had I rented it out, I would have violated the lease conditions, could have been forced to evict the tenants and I could have been penalised with a monetary fine.

Then what felt like an absolute brainwave to me at the time, but probably strikes real estate moguls as property investing 101, was the following: rent is correlated to the number of bedrooms, as is the purchase price, and so what if I could purchase a two-bedroom property at a two-bedroom property price, and then somehow convert it into a three-bedroom property and charge three-bedroom rent? That would definitely boost my rental yield into the 7% plus range. I was aware of the concept of buying a house and turning it into two self-contained flats, but the reason that was not feasible for me is a lot of upfront cash is required to execute that type of conversion. I was thinking along the lines of a simple partition wall splitting either a large bedroom into two, or sectioning part of a living room off. I found a two-bedroom ex-local flat in Stonebridge with a large L-shaped living room, asking price £265K.

The market rent for a three-bedroom flat in that area was £1,750 pcm. There was a lot of demand for this property and the agent was taking sealed bids, which meant every party interested had one shot to make an offer and the highest bid won. I calculated the maximum price I could afford in order to sustain the 7% yield:

MAXIMUM PURCHASE PRICE

$$\frac{\text{Annual Rent}}{\text{Hurdle Rate (\%)}} = \text{Maximum Purchase Price}$$

$$(£1{,}750 \times 12) \,/\, 7\% = £300{,}000$$

I could afford to bid up to £300K for this and so I decided to offer the full £265K. It ranked at the top of all bids and I secured the deal. Ordinarily I would have tried to negotiate, but with the sealed bid curveball I just didn't want to lose out on the investment. It isn't easy to find a flat with a layout that lends itself to an extra bedroom. Not only do you need the space, but also each bedroom has to have a window, has to be of certain dimensions to fit basic furniture like a bed, and has to have a legitimate fire escape. For example, if a room has a small window that one cannot get out of and it does not lead directly onto the hallway, that room does not have a valid fire escape, is deemed inhabitable by regulation and cannot be rented out as a bedroom. Be watchful of this. I recently went to view a three-bed bungalow and left thinking I would make an offer. As I was driving, I was picturing the bedrooms and couldn't for the life of me remember seeing any windows. I went back only to find that not one of the three bedrooms had a window! The layout was such that all of the bedrooms had been built in the centre of the house using internal walls, and surrounding the bedrooms were the kitchen, the living room and the bathroom.

Let's pull together a comprehensive list of things to look out for that influence how profitable and straightforward a transaction will be.

Costs

- A partition wall to section off a legitimate bedroom will increase the rent you can charge.

- Gas central heating is much more cost efficient than electric heating or warm air heating, thus will attract more tenants/higher rent.

- An Energy Performance Certificate (EPC) rating of E+ is required by regulation. All properties being sold on the market will be marketed with an EPC that in essence indicates how costly it is to run a property (heating, electricity, etc). One can improve a low EPC rating by adding loft/floor/wall insulation, switching single-glazed windows to double-glazed, installing a condensing boiler and using low-energy lighting. These action items can rack up expenses, except the relatively cheap to implement low-energy lighting.

- If looking at flats, a long lease keeps the flat at market value and does not detract value. A remaining lease length of 70–80 years is still okay as the property will be mortgageable, but it will cost more to extend the lease due to the marriage value premium so ensure a discount has been priced into the purchase price.

- Damp problems where signs include peeling wallpaper, black spots and mould on walls & ceilings, and a damp smell. Pay particular attention to the upper floor ceiling if the property has a flat roof.

- Small room sizes: sometimes what's marketed as a double bedroom simply because it can fit a double bed is not practically a double bedroom if one cannot add a chest of drawers, a wardrobe, etc. once the bed is in. Bringing it back down to a single bedroom will reduce the rent you can expect. Similarly, ensure that a room marketed as a living/dining room can actually fit a sofa, TV, a dining table and chairs; some investors try to section off part of the living room to create another bedroom, even when there is practically not enough space.

Constraints

- Tenants in situ (tenants that intend to stay and come with the property as opposed to vacant possession). While it can appear helpful to inherit tenants as it saves you the hassle of having to find them yourself, do these tenants pay rent on time, if at all? It's an additional risk and if you end up being unhappy with the tenants, you may have to initiate an eviction process that can sometimes take up to several months, usually accompanied with zero rental income for that period.

- A lease that stipulates you cannot rent out a property – the legal process will unearth this anyway so agents should be upfront about it.

- A property that does not meet standard lending criteria and therefore can only be purchased with cash, e.g. a flat with a short lease. [Refer to 'Lending Criteria' in Property One for a comprehensive list.]

Chain

- A sale with no chain means the property is ready to buy once the legal side is completed. Conversely, imagine you are buying from someone who needs to buy somewhere to live before they can sell and move out. And, imagine whom they are buying from also needs to buy somewhere to live before they can sell and move out. You can see how very easily you could be trapped into a one-year transaction. Longer transactions can be costly from a mortgage perspective, i.e. mortgage offers are only valid for 3–6 months at which point a new application needs to be submitted, thereby incurring a new valuation cost, further credit checks and more admin. Long transactions also present an opportunity cost in that the longer the deposit money stays uninvested, the more one is missing out on prospective rental profit. Therefore, I tend to stick to purchases with no chain.

- No chain and already vacant is something I would even pay a slight premium for. Imagine I'm selling an investment property of mine with no chain. The buyer is ready to move quickly but my tenants won't leave upon the two-month notice period. I would need to enter into an eviction process which could take up to 6–9 months in some London boroughs, and subsequently even though the buyer entered a no-chain transaction, he or she could be stuck in a one-year transaction incurring costs as explained above. No chain and vacant is a personal preference. Some people prefer owner-occupied homes in spite of the chain as the properties tend to be better looked after, and some actually desire a chain as a means to stall time to save up more money and/or delay moving in.

Charges

- Regarding ex-local flats, a section 20 major works bill of less than £10K can be worth paying as the discount you would get on the property could make up for some of the upfront cash outlay. For example, a property is worth £400K but because of a £10K major works bill, you get it for £375K. Working with a 25% deposit, you would have saved £6K on the deposit, £2K in stamp duty, and given your loan would be less you'd probably save approximately £2K in interest repayments over two years. So that £10K would net off. Moreover, you would be banking on the fact that you wouldn't be liable for another major works bill for on average 5–7 years. So, check when the last major works bill was, expect what the next one will be by checking what aspects of the block still need modernising (single-glazing, damaged roof), and corroborate the major works bill with the discount on the purchase price to make sure it is worth paying.

- Properties with a £20K+ section 20 major works bill attached to them – it would depend on your individual cash flow situation, but bear in mind that investors are not permitted to pay these bills in instalments; they need to be settled fully in cash. That much upfront cash could instead be put towards another deposit.

This flat was ex-local but, since it did not have deck-access, was not above commercial premises and was of standard construction, I had access to several lenders. I opted for the following product:

- 80% LTV
- Interest-only
- 3.5% variable over base for two years
- 25-year mortgage term
- £100 application fee
- £350 valuation fee
- 2.5% arrangement fee

Going for an 80% LTV product instead of 75% effectively meant I saved £13,250 on the deposit. I sanity checked whether I could afford the repayments: the base rate was still 0.5% in 2015 meaning my overall interest rate would be 4%; an 80% loan of £212K plus a hefty arrangement fee of £5,300 resulted in monthly repayments of £724.33; with market rents of £1,750 pcm in the area for three-bedroom flats, I felt buffered enough to take on this product.

I completed on the flat in April 2015 and procured tenants paying the full £1,750 pcm. After deducting the mortgage repayment, the service charges and the ground rent from the rental income, I was making an incremental £900 profit a month. Aside from the deposit, I spent £7K on legal fees, stamp duty, mortgage fees, and a partition wall to section off a third bedroom. The full cash outlay was £60K.

Let's summarise the investment:

Property Three	
Purchase price	£265,000
Monthly rent	£1,750
	⇒ Gross yield 8%
Return On Investment	
Cash investment	£60,000
Annual profit	£10,800
	⇒ ROI in 2015 was 18%
Payback Period	
Estimated payback period	6 years
Actual payback period	3 years
Equity released to date	£30,000
Remaining investment	£0
	⇒ ROI since 2018 is ∞

Had I not capitalised on the potential to convert the two-bedroom flat into a three-bed, I would have received an approximate rent of £1,350 pcm and the gross yield would have dropped to 6.1%, hence the investment would not have been viable for me. Furthermore, the reason the refurbishment costs have stayed relatively low for three consecutive purchases is I am very mindful, when choosing between investments, of the aspects that will detract value and cost me to remedy in making the place rentable. These additional costs will affect your overall cash outlay and therefore your return on investment and payback period. More tangibly, any unforeseen refurbishment costs will slow down the process of saving up for the next deposit. Most importantly and something that cannot be stressed enough is, being able to rent out the property quickly is critical to a lucrative buy to let strategy. Everything discussed in this chapter like adequate room sizes, efficient EPC ratings, double-glazing, and so forth – these aspects attract tenants and should be of primary focus when conducting viewings. There is no point buying a bargain property if you're going to struggle to find people that want to live in it!

The aspects discussed in this chapter, however, are only those that we as buyers can observe when looking for opportunities. There are numerous other constraints and charges that could be unearthed during the legal process which would need to either be mitigated, negotiated on, or often they could be enough to pull out from the deal. We'll touch on some of these in Property Four.

To conclude, let's pull out the key takeaways from this chapter:

✓ INCREASING PROPERTY VALUES HAMPER YIELDS
✓ ADJUST YOUR HURDLE RATE IF NECESSARY
✓ IF A PROPERTY IS VERY CHEAP, FIND OUT WHY
✓ TRY TO INCREASE # BEDROOMS TO INCREASE RENT
✓ ENSURE CHOSEN PROPERTY WILL ATTRACT TENANTS

PROPERTY FOUR

A GOOD SOLICITOR GOES A LONG WAY

Spend the Hundreds Now to Save the Thousands Later

I couldn't get my head around the fact that I was essentially paying off someone else's mortgage by renting the place I lived in. By running the numbers I also ascertained that so long as one had the initial deposit for their own home, which I would never have had at this stage had it not been for my first two buy to lets, even capital mortgage repayments were typically cheaper than rent. This presented an imbalance in the market: rent was more expensive than mortgage repayments that could give you the title of a home in twenty-five years! It existed because interest rates were suppressed. In other words, while interest rates remain low, one should try and take advantage of this opportunity.

There was also another driver for owning a residential property that was crucial to my growth strategy. There were lenders on the market that were offering experienced landlords 80–85% LTV mortgages. Since I owned three buy to let properties I was now considered one by most lenders, however in order to access an 85% LTV mortgage, I needed to be an owner-occupant too. If I could start buying properties with only a 15% deposit, I could scale my portfolio that much faster.

While growing my buy to let portfolio with Property Three, I had simultaneously been looking for a residential home. I had £190K in hand. This ordinarily for a buy to let would set the budget at £750–£800K, but it is important to note that for residential mortgages there is an additional criterion one needs to take into account, and that is lenders will typically cap lending at four times your base salary. Let's say I wanted to buy an £800K residential home. With the deposit I had, that would mean I would need to borrow circa £600K and my base salary would need to be £150K at least. It wasn't. So the options laid out to me were to either buy something cheaper or to buy with someone else. My husband and I decided to apply for the mortgage together in our joint names to help maintain the £800K budget.

We wanted a thousand square feet, something that was within a twenty-minute commute to work, and we wanted a flat within a block that had a concierge seeing as both of us worked full-time and were addicted to Amazon deliveries! Turns out there were quite a few options if we included ex-local properties. Layering on our subjective preferences around the type of block we wanted to live in, only three areas suited our budget: Elephant & Castle, Kentish Town and West Hampstead. We walked around all three areas and settled on West Hampstead, which in 2014/15 was a haven for new-build constructions.

Buying a new-build has its pros and cons. To its advantage, if one can manage to buy off-plan, meaning the flat is yet to be built and you are basing the purchase on the location and the architectural plans, it is possible to get a very good discount on the market value. On the flipside, one is buying based on the intention of the developer rather than a finished product, and the difference between what is promised and what is delivered varies among the different development companies. On the plus side, you get to live in a brand new property with full guarantees on appliances, fitted bathrooms and kitchens. On the downside, new-build properties tend to have many minor issues in the first year where you would need to work with the developers to have them resolved. Another big advantage is being able to negotiate add-ons like furniture, or to have input in the actual design of your flat if you buy 'off-plan' enough. The biggest disadvantage for me personally is the financing of a new-build: with most residential properties one can go up to an 85–90% LTV, however most lenders for new-builds cap their products at 75% LTV, some at 80%.

We settled on a three-bedroom off-plan new-build flat that was due to be completed September 2015. The asking price was £925K that we negotiated down to £845K, plus some high-end furniture pieces including fitted wardrobes.

Since we had gone slightly over budget, I applied for a £15K personal loan from my bank. The agreement was to receive an upfront £15K lump sum that would be paid back over twenty-four months with a £600 premium. I welcomed the opportunity to borrow at 2% a year. The money hit my account on the same day. With a confirmed £205K savings account, April 2015 was a month of celebration as we con-firmed the sale by exchanging on our first residential home. I'm afraid that really was the peak though and things went downhill from there because of one thing and one thing only – our solicitor.

One of the provisos of getting the deal done was to use the solicitor that the estate agent was recommending, as she had been conducting all the conveyancing on the other sales in the block and already had most of the information she needed to transact quickly. I went to meet her and the exchange of the property went through absolutely fine. It entailed basic ID checks, confirming with a mortgage broker that I would have no issue securing a mortgage, going through the plans of the flat to ensure I understood and was happy with the proposed structure, and paying 10% to exchange on the property. Having researched a little about new-build properties and discovering that only a fraction get delivered on time, I incorporated a stipulation into the contract: if the completion notice is not served by 30 April 2016, the contract will be null and void and the deposit will be refunded. This essentially meant incorporating a longstop date to avoid the deal dragging on. It also meant we could manage our rental contract in the interim.

September 2015 came and went with no completion notice. Our rental lease also came to an end September 2015 and we didn't know whether to extend for another six months or whether the completion notice could be served any day then, at which point I would be liable to complete within ten working days. It caused all sorts of problems – we needed more time than that to secure a mortgage, and getting one in advance was a waste of money if it was only going to lapse in 3–6 months anyway. I went to see the construction and even though the new delivery date they were then proposing was November 2015, the block looked far from ready. I bided my time on submitting a mortgage application and ending the rental lease.

As we entered Feb/March 2016, I had still heard nothing. Countless calls to my solicitor were unreturned, emails were not responded to... I wanted to understand the repercussions of missing the longstop date. Were there any? The fact that I was dealing directly with a partner at the law firm seemed to also mean nothing. Finally, I managed to get hold of her, and she stated very clearly, "I'm not sure what happens, the developer's solicitors are ignoring me, I'll come back to you".

The agent that sold me the flat had also left the estate agency and so I resorted to hounding the developers directly. They at long last responded to me with a proposed new longstop date, 30 June 2016. I signed an addendum to the contract agreeing to this and decided that should this deadline be breached, I'd pull out of the deal.

I worked with my broker to apply for a mortgage with a lender that was offering an 80% LTV product on a new-build. They thankfully issued a residential mortgage offer:

- 80% LTV
- Capital and interest repayment[15]
- 1.89% fixed for two years
- 35-year mortgage term
- £800 valuation fee
- No arrangement or application fee

Two months ensued again of me leaving missed calls, voice-mails and emails to the solicitor. About one in ten were answered. As we approached the 30th June, I could not get hold of anyone, not the developers, nor my solicitor. I wanted to understand our rights. I had no idea what would happen after the deadline and I now wanted to pull out of the deal. I left a voicemail for my solicitor stating very clearly, "please call me, I want a refund on the flat".

The 30th June came and went. On the 7th July, I finally got the call from my solicitor saying the completion notice had been served. I retaliated with a barrage of questions around her lack of response and concluded with confirming that I had pulled out of the deal. She then said that she hadn't relayed this to the developers, because she thought my message had been left in frustration (!), and since the completion notice had now been served, I would be in breach of contract if I tried to pull out!

I remained in the deal primarily because I had no choice, but also because since I had exchanged, a new tax rule had come out that meant anyone who now purchased a second

---

15   Interest-only was not available at 80% LTV

property would owe an additional 3% stamp duty tax. Using the stamp duty calculator on the Buy To Let Loose app, you can see that at a purchase price of £845K, I would have owed £32,250 had I exchanged before 25 November 2015.[16] If I now went for another property at the same purchase price, I'd owe almost double that amount with a stamp duty tax bill of £57,600!

I went to see the block and it was still far from complete. Yes, we could live inside the flat but there was no concierge, no reception desk, no front door to the building and a building site at the back where we were meant to have land-scaped gardens. I decided to approach the developer and use the state of the block as leverage to renegotiate. Having spoken to some of the workmen on site, I concluded that the lack of progress was down to a constraint in their liquidity. You see, technically I was contractually bound to pay the £845K and they did not have to negotiate at all, however, to be tied up in a litigation case would have taken too long for them to get the money they needed and so I took a chance. I managed to knock off £75K to end at a final purchase price of £770K. I was ecstatic! The meaningful reduction meant I'd save a cash sum of £18,750 (£15K from a lower deposit and £3,750 from a lower stamp duty liability). Because of the change in price, we had the mortgage offer amended.

Then, on 15 July 2016, the morning of planned completion of the sale, I got a call from the partner solicitor saying the following:

---

16   The cut-off date set by the UK government

"Hi, Anshu. Good news, we are ready to complete, we just need an additional £4,350 from you."

"Err, I think there's some sort of misunderstanding, I should be receiving £18,750 cash from the completion money we have sent you given the price reduction!"

"The thing is, you now owe an additional 3% in stamp duty as when you changed the price of the flat, I changed the contract and so technically, you exchanged after 25 November 2015."

I was shell-shocked. I went on to accuse their firm of incompetence and their excuse was, "It's a new ruling and so we haven't come across this before." The other excuse that I found hilarious was, "I've been on holiday and there was no one that understood the case in my absence to relay the information to you."

I called my usual solicitor to seek advice, and he confirmed that we would now owe the additional 3% given the solicitor had changed the contract. What he also told me was that by adding a £75K allowance clause, the contract change could have been circumvented. I then called another solicitor that my colleague recommended who independently said exactly the same thing. The additional 3% stamp duty could have been completely avoided had my solicitor known what she was doing!

I was forced to complete by contract law, didn't receive the £19K refund and instead had to fork out an extra £4K. I promised myself to only ever use my trusted legal advisors going forward. One realises very quickly that there is nothing really in place to protect us from getting bad advice, either from your mortgage broker or from your lawyer. I mean needless to say I looked into suing the law firm (still ongoing), but at the end of the day, I'm still £23K out of pocket at present because I didn't have good legal representation.

It will take time to build rapport with a good solicitor unless someone can recommend one to you, but I outline the general service that should be provided, followed by a few tips to ensure your solicitor is on the ball, and for completeness an overview of general costs incurred when buying a property.

The Standard Legal Process

- The estate agent will send out the memorandum of sale to both sets of solicitors outlining the sale agreement including the purchase price, details of both solicitors, and details of both the buyer (you or your company) and the seller.

- The seller's solicitor will issue a draft contract to your solicitor.

- Local searches will be conducted by your solicitor and can include environmental, drainage and local authority searches.

- Your solicitor will raise enquiries that will need to be satisfied by the seller's solicitor.

- Once you solicitor is satisfied with all responses, both parties will exchange contracts and you will pay (traditionally) 10% of the purchase price in order to secure the deal. After exchange, you will be liable for the property and will forfeit the 10% deposit paid should you forfeit the transaction.

- Your solicitor will request for the mortgage funds to be drawn down from your lender (usually takes 3–5 business days).

- Your solicitor will issue you with a completion statement that will outline all outstanding monies that you will need to transfer (the remaining deposit, stamp duty, legal fees). Upon completion, you own the property and can collect the keys.

- Post-completion, your solicitor will submit a stamp duty land tax return and pay the stamp duty tax for you, and they will update the Land Registry title deed with its new ownership – you.

A Few Tips

- All lenders have a panel of solicitors they will work with.

Check your solicitor's firm is indeed on the panel of your chosen lender, otherwise, you may need to pay for dual representation (your existing lawyer and one from the lender's panel).

- If you are buying a vacant property, consider exchanging and completing on the same day, or at least minimise the time in between. Once you exchange on a property, you are bound to buying the property. Vacant properties are easy targets for squatters and vandalism. Should your property fall victim to this in between exchange and completion, you will have no leverage to persuade the seller to sort the situation and will have to complete.

- Once solicitors conduct all the searches, they go through the reports and put forward comments and red flags for your attention. Depending on how good your solicitor is, there are things they can also miss. They partly cover themselves by sending you the reports so that you can let them know if you have any concerns. Really read through all the documents – the lease conditions, the environmental searches, confirm the plot you are buying on the Ordnance Survey that your lawyer will provide you with. Remember, you have seen the property and negotiated the terms, not your solicitor.

- For flat purchases, ensure your solicitor gets an under-taking from the seller to state they will cover all service charges owed up until the day of completion. The last thing you want is to buy a flat that comes with £1K per annum service charges, only to find that the last three years haven't been paid where the bill now falls to you.

- When transferring money across to solicitors for exchange and completion, ensure you get the bank details verbally and not over email. I recently had been liaising with my solicitor on a purchase over email, only to find that the preceding seven days worth of email correspondence had been with a fraudster! I was on the verge of transferring £66K to a hacker's account, and thankfully I had the better sense to call my lawyer to query why the account details were different to the ones I usually paid into.

- Ask your solicitor to conduct a chancel repair liability search. There is a very old law in place that could enforce property owners to contribute to the repairs of the chancel of the local parish church. It is highly unlikely but completely plausible, and so if your property does fall in the vicinity of being potentially charged, speak to your solicitor about insurance.

- If you are buying a house, you will typically need to show proof of buildings insurance before the lender will release the mortgage funds. The actual insurance can be commissioned on the day, but you may want to start researching the various insurers in advance. Furthermore, you are liable for insurance from the day you exchange, not complete. Please note that for flats within a block, the buildings insurance is usually covered within the annual service charges so do not double up.[17]

General Costs

- Get an upfront quote of what will be charged. A typical fee schedule from a solicitor looks something like the following:

FEES	
Professional fee	£799.00
Acting on behalf of lender fee	£175.00
Completing stamp duty land tax (SDLT) transaction return	£75.00
Administrative costs of arranging bank telegraphic transfer	£35.00
Anti-money laundering (AML) checks	£16.79
Sub-total	1,100.79
VAT @ 20%	£220.16
Total fees	£1,320.95

17   Check the detail of your specific service charges – if buildings insurance is not included, please arrange cover.

PLUS DISBURSEMENTS	
Searches (approx.) [local authority, environmental, drainage]	£350.00
Bankruptcy search (VAT exempt)	£2.00
Land Registry search (VAT exempt)	£3.00
Stamp duty tax liability (VAT exempt)	depends
Land registration fee (VAT exempt)	depends
Chancel indemnity policy	£20.00

Some of the legal fees will most likely be required at the outset of the legal proceedings, much like a retainer, and the balance upon completion.

- The deposit money will be required upon completion, specific to the LTV of your mortgage product.

- The stamp duty money will be required upon completion.[18] If you are a first-time buyer purchasing a residential home for £500K or less, or if you are buying a property to replace your main residence, please seek professional advice from your mortgage broker or solicitor because you could be eligible for stamp duty (part) exemption.

- The money required for refurbishment won't be needed

---

18 You can use the Stamp Duty calculator on the Buy To Let Loose app to determine exactly how much you would owe for any given buy to let purchase.

until after completion, so it is okay if this takes a little extra time to save up. However, the longer it takes to amass, the longer your property will remain untenanted and all the while you will continue paying the monthly mortgage repayments.

- Mortgage costs such as the valuation fee, any broker fee and/or application fees will be due throughout the process, pre-completion; arrangement fees can be added to the loan amount or paid upfront.

- Miscellaneous costs like a section 20 major works bill will need to be paid in full and in cash, post-completion; a lease extension that is part of the transaction will need to be paid for pre-completion; some buyers use a service to identify good property investments, in which case a finders fee could be due post-exchange.

[You can use the Buying Property calculator on the Buy To Let Loose app to budget these costs and sum up the amount of cash you will need for a specific investment.]

Our residential home completed in July 2016. Property values had increased a lot since we exchanged in April 2015. Using Zoopla to guesstimate, the flat had increased in value by 30% in just over a year and was now worth £1m. The first thing that sprung to mind, true to form, was – how could I release some equity? The refinancing option was not due for another two years but I didn't want to wait that long, especially given Brexit had been announced and I had no idea if that £1m would hold its value for two years. Another option to exploit the increase in value was to sell the property: unlike buy to let properties where we have said releasing equity can be preferential to selling in order to avoid the capital gains tax, the home you live in is your principal residence and exempt from capital gains tax upon selling. However, I have a strong view that the flat will increase further in value over the long-term and ruled that option out.

I spoke directly to the lender about a further advance. It turned out that if I waited six months, I could instruct a new valuation and if there was equity to release, I could take out a mini mortgage with its own terms instead of having to wait the full two years.

In December I started preparing. It was like a standard mortgage application where once again credit checks were applied, proof of income was checked and a valuation took place. Fortunately, the surveyor agreed with the £1m figure I had opined. The lender was willing to lend up to 75% of the new value, which meant there was £134K remaining loan amount available:[19]

Current loan amount = 80% of £770K = £616K
Available loan amount = 75% of £1m = £750K
Remaining loan amount = £750K – £616K = £134K

---

19   These calculations are inbuilt into the Releasing Equity calculator on the Buy To Let Loose app.

I released £134K in January 2017. The repayment schedule for this further advance was £400 a month for the next twenty-four months, which equalled just shy of £10K. I subtracted £10K from the equity release and put that into a savings account to take care of the additional interest every month. Why? Because my residential home wasn't earning any rental income to cover this increase in cash outflow.

Having used the full £190K savings, the £15K HSBC loan, and some of my salary in clearing up the solicitor's mess, this further advance was a saving grace: out of the £207K cash outlay, I had two-thirds of it back in six months to put to work again! What made it such a good investment? We got a good price due to the off-plan aspect, West Hampstead was undergoing a lot of regeneration with new-build flats, popular restaurants and supermarkets quickly lining the local high street, and it is, without doubt, one of the most accessible areas in London with easy access to the Thameslink, the Tube and the Overground.

If your living criteria aren't matching the good investment areas, think outside the box to kill two birds with one stone. Why can't you buy in a good investment area, is it too expensive? Can you sub-let a room? Or do you really want to live in a particular area because you have friends and family residing there, despite the fact there is no catalyst that could help lift property prices in the area? If you have reason to settle in an area that doesn't present a good investment opportunity but you know it will be a permanent base for you, yes you could still consider buying as opposed to renting for that additional security. However, if this is simply a place 'for now', consider holding off the residential mortgage for the time being and instead using your deposit to buy a good investment somewhere. You could then use the rental income from that investment to rent temporarily in the area you want to live in. The advantage is at least the good investment property can more likely appreciate in value and you would be able to release equity to continue growing your property portfolio.

Let's summarise the investment:

Property Four	
Purchase price	£770,000
Monthly rent	N/A
	⇒ Gross yield N/A
Return On Investment[20]	
Cash investment	£207,000
Annual profit	N/A
	⇒ ROI N/A
Payback Period[21]	
Estimated payback period	N/A
Actual payback period	N/A
Equity released to date	£134,000
Remaining investment	£73,000
	⇒ ROI N/A

20   The ROI is not applicable since there is no rental income.

The three positive aspects of this investment are:

1. The mortgage repayment is less than the rent I was paying, which has lessened my monthly cash outflow.
2. By paying capital and interest repayments, I am also working towards eventually owning my home. Another way to look at this is even more of my salary income is being converted into capital that I can't spend; capital and interest mortgages are an excellent mechanism to save money.
3. Having gotten the majority of the cash outlay back after six months has been critical in growing my buy to let portfolio, as we will observe in Properties Five – Eight.

To conclude, let's pull out the key takeaways from this chapter:

✓ ACQUIRE GREAT ADVISORS, GET RECOMMENDATIONS
✓ ENSURE SOLICITOR IS ON MOST LENDER PANELS
✓ GET LEGAL FEE QUOTE IN ADVANCE AND IN WRITING
✓ QUESTION LEGAL ADVICE, DO NOT FOLLOW BLINDLY
✓ IF YOU CAN AFFORD A RESIDENTIAL HOME, BUY ONE
✓ TREAT IT LIKE AN INVESTMENT, RELEASE EQUITY

---

21 The estimated payback period is not applicable since the investment does not pay back any money. However, in time if I am able to release enough equity from the residential home and pay back all of the cash invested, an actual payback period will materialise.

PROPERTY FIVE

SETTING UP A LIMITED COMPANY

To Incorporate or Not to Incorporate, That Is the Question

With the UK government enforcing laws left, right and centre to limit the profit landlords are making, it is critical to be tax efficient with your investments. Up until 2017, buy to let mortgage interest could be offset as an expense against rental income. For example, if you owned a property that was earning £10K a year in rent and your interest-only mortgage repayments were £3K a year, only the £7K of profit would be subject to tax. This is no longer the case. For anyone that falls within the basic rate tax band, the new tax ruling put forth in the 2016 Budget may not affect you; higher and additional rate taxpayers, however, could be severely impacted.[22]

To refresh, here are the current tax bands for 2018/19:

---

22   As of 2018/19 and specific to UK tax-domiciled individuals.

Band	Taxable Income	Tax Rate
Personal Allowance[23]	Up to £11,850	0%
Basic Rate	£11,851–£46,350	20%
Higher Rate	£46,351–£150,000	40%
Additional Rate	Over £150,000	45%
Corporate Rate	Any	19%

This means that if you, through employment or other means, have a gross income in excess of £46,351, any profits you make on property you own or buy will now be affected. Instead of being able to claim the full mortgage interest as an expense, you will only be able to claim part of it, the same amount that a basic rate taxpayer is claiming. That is, everyone will receive the same amount of tax credit at 20pc.

To illustrate, if you were a basic rate taxpayer, had been earning £10K a year in rent and paying £3K of mortgage interest a year, you would have owed 20% tax on the £7K profit, i.e. £1,400 (assuming you had no other deductible expenses to claim). Now the entire £10K of rental income would be subject to 20% tax (£2K), less the 20pc credit (20% of £3K mortgage interest = £600), which again gives us the same £1,400 due. In other words, nothing will change if you still remain a basic rate taxpayer after incorporating all rental income.

If you were a higher rate taxpayer in the same situation, you would have also been liable to pay tax on the £7K profit

---

23   You don't get a personal allowance if your taxable income over £123,700.

but at 40%, hence you would have owed £2,800 in tax. Now the entire £10K of rental income would be subject to tax but at 40% (£4K), less the 20pc credit (20% of £3K mortgage interest = £600), which gives an increased tax liability of £3,400.

Why should higher rate and additional rate taxpayers pay significant attention to this? It is not just because one will now pay more tax, which in itself can obviously be a deterrent to buy to let. The fundamental difference is previously one would only pay tax on profits and therefore if one was paying tax, by default they were making a profit. Now it is possible that one could be hit with a tax bill that eats away all the profit and leaves behind a loss-making investment!

To show an example of this, let's keep the annual rent at £10K and increase the hypothetical mortgage interest per annum to £8K. A higher rate taxpayer ordinarily would have had to pay 40% tax on the £2K profit, which equates to £800 tax and £1,200 residual profit. Per the new ruling, 40% of the entire rent would be due (£4K) less the 20pc credit (20% of £8K = £1,600), which equals £2,400. But if you are getting £10K a year, paying £8K in mortgage interest and paying a £2,400 tax bill, all of a sudden you are left with a deficit of £400 per annum, a loss-making investment.

In actuality, the tax ruling of the 20pc tax credit being standardised across all individual tax brackets is being phased: 50% of the mortgage interest can still be offset in this tax year,[24] 25% next year, and none of it by the tax year

---

24   This phasing nuance is inbuilt into the Monthly Profit calculator on the Buy To Let Loose app.

commencing April 2020. But given we have clear direction as to where things are heading, I decided to seek advice in order to set up a tax-efficient strategy to manage this change.

It is necessary for me to categorically state here that it is paramount for each individual to get his or her own tax advice, and to seek advice from a professional mortgage broker. The advice given to you will depend on your own personal circumstances, e.g. your tax domicile, your income, your credit history, the number of properties you own, the type of properties you want to buy, your current and future liquidity requirements, etc. The strategy recommended to me by my advisors was to set up a limited company and to purchase all future buy to let properties in it. Let's discuss the advantages and the disadvantages of doing this, specific to buy to let:

Advantages of Limited Companies

- Mortgage interest can be fully claimed as an expense (not just the 20pc) resulting in lower reported profits for higher and additional rate taxpayers, thus lower tax bills.

- All profits will be subject to corporation tax at 19% rather than income tax, so very beneficial if you are a higher or additional rate taxpayer at 40% or 45%. If you are a basic rate taxpayer, this advantage is negligible.

- A tax-free dividend of £2K per shareholder per year can be taken out of the company – the company is allowed at most four shareholders.

- The rental stress tests (affordability checks) are not as strict for a company as they are now for individual purchasers. Therefore it is easier for properties to surpass some of the lending criteria when bought in a company. [We will introduce rental stress tests in Property Seven.]

Disadvantages of Limited Companies

- There are a limited number of lenders that offer buy to let mortgages to companies.

- Mortgage products are more expensive when the applicant is a company as opposed to an individual.[25] As the trend to buy in a company increases, the difference in interest rates is narrowing but still remains on average 1%.

- If you want to extract more than the tax-free dividend, it will cost you to take this additional money out of

---

25   There is a caveat to this, and that is when the lender is a specialist lender that targets company applicants. A specialist lender may have cheaper mortgage products for companies than they do for individuals, but those cheaper company products will still be more expensive than individual products across the whole market.

the company as you would need to first pay the usual 19% corporation tax, and then you would have to pay dividend tax on top:[26]

- 7.5% for basic rate taxpayers
- 32.5% for higher rate taxpayers
- 38.1% for additional rate taxpayers

- There are frictional costs to setting up a company (a couple of hundred pounds), plus lots of admin including setting up a business bank account, filing a separate tax return every year, and filing minutes after every key decision, transaction and meeting.

- There is no tax-free personal allowance for a company, currently at £11,850 for individuals.

- The types of properties one can buy in a company are limited. For example, to buy an ex-local flat that has deck-access is exceptionally difficult to do in a company because there are only a handful of lenders that would even consider it. One would have to forgo some good yielding investment opportunities.

- You would need to be a guarantor of the company loan. Therefore all credit checks would still take place in your name like it would for a mortgage in your personal

---

26   As of 2018/19

name. Not a disadvantage as such, but important to mention in case one thinks about transacting in a company to avoid personal scrutiny.

At this point in time, I owned three buy to let properties in my personal name. My approximate annual income on the three properties was:

• Shepherd's Bush Flat	£23,000
• Harlesden Flat	£16,000
• Stonebridge Flat	£21,000
	£60,000

My corporate salary took me out of the basic rate tax band so all three flats would be subject to the new ruling. However, if I were to stop earning, most of my rental income would consequently fall into the basic tax bracket (up to £46,350), if not all after claiming deductible expenses like maintenance, the 20pc tax credit and annual service charges.

I had more recently been considering the timing of when I would make my next move. I had always planned that when I reached four buy to let properties and an annual rental income of circa £80K, I would cut loose and venture into the startup world. However, with this new ruling in place that would eat into my profits come tax year commencing 6 April 2017, I instead set 31 March 2017 as my deadline to quit so that the new tax year would be clear of any salary income.

It was January 2017, I had £124K in hand from the equity release of my residential home and I wanted to put that money to work. Now in order to get a mortgage offer, one needs to typically provide the last three months of payslips. Once I left my job, I knew it would restrict the number of lenders I could access; many do not count rent towards income and therefore I wouldn't even meet the £25K minimum income criterion these lenders typically assert. That gave me three months to find, negotiate and get mortgage offers on as many properties that would utilise the £124K.

I more or less agreed with my tax advisor that in spite of giving up my salary, it still made sense for me to buy future properties within a limited company. The three properties in my own name were using up my personal allowance and they were also making the most of my lower rate tax band. After deductible expenses, with any luck, I would remain a basic rate taxpayer and cap tax liabilities at 20% of profits. Then with any future properties bought in a company, I would be able to cap tax liabilities at 19% of profits. My only real concern was that I needed some of the rental income that was to come from the company's future properties to live off, and the £2K tax-free dividend a year wasn't going to be enough. What's the point of saving a larger proportion of profits within a company, only to have to pay tax should one want to take it out and spend it!

I voiced this concern to my tax advisor who in turn offered a solution. He advised that I 'loan' the £124K to the company.

I could then call upon that loan as and when I needed to with no tax implications (unless I charged my company interest on the loan, in which case I would be adding to my personal income). He further advised that uncalled profits should roll up in the company to fund future purchases. I figured that the £124K loan recall, the tax-free dividend a year, the rental income I was getting from my personal name properties plus any equity I could potentially release from them would all together sustain me for at least a few years. Thereafter... well, to try and conjure up what income tax bands and rules will be, at what rate corporation tax will be, what government will be in seat and if the wind will still be against landlords is a futile task as it's anyone's guess.

The final sanity check I did was to run the numbers on how much profit I would make if I bought my next purchase in my own name versus if I went down the company route. I assumed a repeat purchase of Property Three and used the same numbers accordingly, and I assumed I would no longer have a salary:

Personal

Annual Rent	£21,000
Less Tax Due @ 40%	(£8,400)
Less Mortgage Interest	(£8,692)
Plus 20pc Tax Credit	£1,738.40
Annual Net Profit	**£5,646.40**

Company

Annual Rent	£21,000
Less Mortgage Interest	(£10,865)[27]
	£10,135
Less Tax Due @ 19%	(£1,925.65)
Annual Net Profit	**£8,209.35**

This hypothetical but very likely scenario highlights the benefit of being able to fully expense mortgage interest rather than subjecting the entire rental income to tax and receiving a 20pc credit, and it also draws attention to the fact that even after fully expensing mortgage interest, companies still get to pay less than half the rate of higher and additional rate taxpayers. In monetary terms, an additional £2.5K a year could be saved by buying in a company. I decided to proceed down the limited company route.

There are a couple of ways to set up a company, namely to do it yourself for a fraction of the cost, or to pay an accountant or tax advisor to do it for you for about £200. I opted for the latter to ensure it was the right type of vehicle that was being incorporated and with the right SIC codes (they define what your company does). This will be critical when it comes to mortgage applications as the lenders that do offer mortgages to companies only do so to certain types of structures. I set up a non-trading limited company with the following SIC codes:

---

27   I have assumed the mortgage interest rate for a company would be 1% more expensive, per the rationale outlined in the disadvantages of buying in a limited company.

- **68209** – other letting & operating of own or leased real estate
- **68100** – buying and selling of own real estate

In terms of shareholder structure, there was a trade-off to be made: if I added another shareholder, it would mean double the tax-free dividends a year could be declared, but that shareholder would then need to be involved in all company mortgage applications meaning double the admin for me, double the credit checks and double the risk of finding possible reasons to not lend to me. I decided to be the sole shareholder of the company, for now at least.

Next came a business bank account. I chose my incumbent bank to house the account in order to speed up the process, given they had most of the information they needed already. All in all, it took one month to incorporate my company and a corresponding bank account.

Meanwhile, I had started hunting for property investments. Conducting as many viewings as I had in north-west London, I had build rapport with a couple of estate agents who I called upon. There was a property for sale in Willesden, a three-bed ex-local flat with deck-access. Adding salt to the wound in terms of likelihood of getting a mortgage, it was also a six-storey building. Plus points were it had a lift, was of standard construction and had a ninety-year lease. I wanted to write it off but I was getting a fantastic price on it at £319K, and coupled with the agent promising me he could get £1,900 pcm rent, the return was hitting my 7% hurdle rate:

GROSS YIELD

$$\frac{\text{Annual Rent}}{\text{Purchase Price}} = \text{Gross Yield (\%)}$$

£22,800 / £319,000 = 7.1%

It had taken so much time and effort to unearth a 7% yielding property with my last buy to let, due to valuations skyrocketing (and still high), that I found myself almost immediately accepting the deal.

Cue my mortgage broker. He had all of my details, knew my working style and my preferences on products, hence the relationship had become a very efficient one. It was also an honest one. My broker conveyed his reservations around the ability to buy these sorts of flats in a company and that it would be a hit and miss approach in trying to secure a mortgage on this flat. Not only would it waste time, I would lose any valuation and processing fees were the applications rejected. Alas, I didn't want to let the opportunity go without a clear – "we will not get a mortgage" – so I decided to proceed with the mortgage application but conservatively held off the solicitors from doing any work (and therefore incurring costs) until a mortgage offer was on the table.

As it is, there were only a handful of lenders that allowed company applicants at the time:

1. Aldermore
2. Kent Reliance
3. Precise
4. Paragon
5. Metro Bank
6. National Counties Building Society
7. Axis
8. Shawbrook
9. Vida
10. Newbury Building Society
11. Buckinghamshire Building Society
12. State Bank of India
13. Fleet Mortgages

Out of these, only Aldermore, Kent Reliance, Precise, Axis, Shawbrook and Vida were considering ex-local properties with deck-access, and that too on a case-by-case basis. My broker and I decided to try for a fairly competitive 80% LTV product and only needed the ex-local block to be majority privately owned. I logged a request with Brent Council to inform me of the percentage.

The mortgage application process was near enough identical to applying in one's personal name, essentially because I am the sole shareholder of the company. It did not matter that my company had zero history for the company was still bracketed as an experienced landlord, thanks to my personal status.

After paying £650 in valuation fees, the lender rejected

my company's application on the basis of the surveyor's comments stating that the majority of the block was still council owned. Meanwhile, I had gotten confirmation from Brent Council that the block was in fact 60% privately owned. Relaying that back to the lender surprisingly made no difference as their decision had been made.

Despite being out of pocket, I wanted to attempt one more application. Instead of choosing the most competitive product, I asked my broker which potential lender he had a strong inside connect to. I took advantage of that relationship and asked him to proactively disclose to the lender that the block is 60% privately owned. The lender agreed to consider my application. The good news was, thanks to the positive notes my broker's contact added to the case, they agreed to lend on the flat. The not so good news was, they would cap the lending at 75% LTV.

With a purchase price of £319K, I was looking at a deposit of £80K plus £15.5K in stamp duty (including the additional 3% charge). Incorporating legal costs, a slight renovation and the mortgage application fees, it required an even £100K cash outlay.

I opted for the following product:

- 75% LTV
- Interest-only
- 3.39% fixed for two years
- 25-year mortgage term
- £150 application fee

- £600 valuation fee
- 1.5% arrangement fee

I completed on the flat and procured tenants that paid £1,863 pcm, so slightly less than the £1,900 the agent had promised but still achieving a 7% return. After deducting the mortgage repayment, the service charges and the ground rent from the rental income, I was making an incremental £1K profit a month.

Let's summarise the investment:

Property Five	
Purchase price	£319,000
Monthly rent	£1,863
	⇒ Gross yield 7%
Return On Investment	
Cash investment	£100,000
Annual profit	£12,000
	⇒ ROI in 2017 was 12%
Payback Period	
Estimated payback period	8 years
Actual payback period	TBD
Equity released to date	£0
Remaining investment[28]	£85,000
	⇒ ROI in 2018 is 14%

28 Even though I haven't released any equity yet, I have been earning rental profits from the property to pay back my cash investment.

£100K felt like a lot to put into one investment property but in order to remove the emotional bias, I simply reverted to the hurdle rate I had set myself. This investment met the desired return and so it got the green light. However, given I only had £24K left to invest, I needed to find opportunities requiring far less of a deposit. London was out of the game. It was time to seek out investment opportunities outside of the capital, as we will encounter in Property Six.

To conclude, let's pull out the key takeaways from this chapter:

✓ QUALIFIED TAX ADVICE IS VITAL, BUT BROADLY ...
✓ ... BASIC RATE TAXPAYERS CAN BUY IN OWN NAME
✓ ... HIGHER RATE TAXPAYERS CONSIDER A COMPANY
✓ SET UP CORRECT COMPANY STRUCTURE & SIC CODES
✓ SET UP A CORRESPONDING BUSINESS BANK ACCOUNT
✓ LOAN FUNDS TO COMPANY ON INTEREST-FREE BASIS
✓ UTILISE TAX-FREE DIVIDENDS EVERY YEAR
✓ FILE A SEPARATE COMPANY TAX RETURN ANNUALLY

PROPERTY SIX

LOCATION, LOCATION, LOCATION

Commuter Hubs Are the New London

The biggest attraction to investing in London is the capital appreciation. It plays an integral part in my growth strategy since this is what allows me to release equity and further invest. Although given the elevated valuation levels, it appeared as though I had ridden the London curve for long enough. I needed to identify areas where property prices had yet to spike.

It was February 2017, I had handed in my notice, and I had £24K left of the equity release from my residential home. Separately, while I had been unable to save any of my base salary since Property Three (largely due to the MBA loan repayments; an increased rental prior to buying a residential home and now a capital repayment mortgage; and payments for a wedding that went way over budget!), I had continued to save every penny of the rental income from Properties One – Three over the last two years in a savings account, which now amounted to a sum of £40K.

I live in West Hampstead and use the Thameslink to travel in and out of the city. I had been so accustomed to using the Tube, I was amazed to learn how fast the trains are and just how quickly one could travel into London from places like St Albans, Luton, Brighton, Bedford. I appreciate that getting to other cities like Birmingham, Manchester, Edinburgh and Glasgow is also pretty seamless, but for my first out of London property, I wanted somewhere close by in order to frequently conduct viewings and to still be able to use my London builders for the renovations and maintenance.

I identified five commuter hubs where one could still buy a house for less than £200K. I then spent the next four consecutive weekends conducting back-to-back viewings and speaking to agents to better understand the areas, the rental market and demand, and any catalysts in the areas that could prompt significant capital appreciation. The five areas I explored are:

- Milton Keynes
- Northampton
- Kettering
- Bedford
- Luton

I really liked Milton Keynes from an investment perspective because it is less than an hour's drive or a 30–40 minute train ride from London, and moreover it has plenty of job opportunities with many companies having a local presence there. Northampton, a little further out but still within an hour from London by train, has an existing university with a new campus opening up in the town centre. I got comfortable with the rental demand there. What I wasn't a fan of is how far some of the residential areas are from the central station – it's very much a driver's town. Kettering had very affordable homes, and it was indeed accessible with a direct train, but it felt like I was unnecessarily going too far afield when good opportunities existed closer to London. Bedford was interesting – it is in proximity to these other commuter hubs with similar types of properties, yet the asking prices were notably higher. I didn't spend enough time there to understand why, again because there were better yielding opportunities in Milton Keynes and Northampton. And finally Luton, the closest commuter hub to London, had already experienced significant capital appreciation; I believe I've missed the boat on this one. I decided to focus my efforts on Milton Keynes.

Seeing as all property investment purchases would now be undertaken in my company, I wanted to change tack a little. I wanted to go for properties that would have no difficulty in getting a mortgage, given the lender pool for companies is already a lot smaller. That meant excluding ex-local flats and non-standard construction properties from my search completely. Turns out that Milton Keynes is a non-standard construction haven and avoiding that aspect was a lot easier said than done since many agents just did not know the difference! A flat roof, for example, technically constitutes non-standard construction, and we can see this for ourselves, but the composition of the walls – concrete, brick, timber – is not so easy to detect. My advice is, do not rely on the agent's comments and check the Energy Performance Certificate. To illustrate:

Energy Efficiency Rating

	Current	Potential
Very energy efficient - lower running costs		
(92 plus) A		
(81-91) B		◄86
(69-80) C		
(55-68) D		
(39-54) E	◄47	
(21-38) F		
(1-20) G		
Not energy efficient - higher running costs		

Summary of this home's energy performance related features

Element	Description	Energy Efficiency
Walls	Solid brick, as built, no insulation (assumed)	★ ☆ ☆ ☆ ☆
Roof	Pitched, no insulation	★ ☆ ☆ ☆ ☆
Floor	Suspended, no insulation (assumed)	—
Windows	Fully double glazed	★ ★ ★ ☆ ☆
Main heating	Boiler and radiators, mains gas	★ ★ ★ ★ ☆
Main heating controls	Programmer and room thermostat	★ ★ ★ ☆ ☆
Secondary heating	None	—
Hot water	From main system	★ ★ ★ ★ ☆
Lighting	Low energy lighting in all fixed outlets	★ ★ ★ ★ ★

Overall this property has a very low energy efficiency rating of E47 and it could be difficult to let as it is at the bottom end of the minimum 'E' rating now required by regulation for any tenancy agreement. The important elements to note in the first instance are the ones the lenders are interested in, namely solid brick + pitched roof = standard construction. Check. Please note it is the 'no insulation' in both of these elements that results in a very poor performance rating, not the fact that it is standard construction. By adding insulation, the rating would meaningfully increase.

Having conducted a dozen viewings and sifted through a dozen more EPCs, I found a three-bedroom ex-local house of standard construction, asking price £170K. The expected rent on the house was £950 pcm. This set the maximum purchase price I could pay at just over £162K:

MAXIMUM PURCHASE PRICE

$$\frac{\text{Annual Rent}}{\text{Hurdle Rate (\%)}} = \text{Maximum Purchase Price}$$

$$£11,400 / 7\% = £162,857$$

It was already vacant and they wanted a quick sale, as did I. I managed to negotiate down to £160K on the basis that I would complete within a month. I immediately had my mortgage broker apply for the following product:

- 85% LTV
- Interest-only
- 4.39% variable (linked to the lender's standard variable rate)
- 25-year mortgage term
- £150 application fee
- £450 valuation fee
- 2.5% arrangement fee
- No early repayment charge (ERC)

I opted for an 85% LTV product so that I could minimise my cash outlay and save up that much faster for the next purchase. The quid pro quo was obviously the high monthly interest repayments that worked out to £510, incorporating the larger than usual arrangement fee (which, per my standard practice, I added to the loan amount). The additional benefit of no ERCs – typically you would have to pay something like 3% of the loan in year one and 2% in year two as a penalty if you wanted to remortgage before the initial period was up – meant that I could essentially remortgage the product whenever I wanted to. This feature was especially critical. If you note, the product is variable but not linked to the base rate that is set by the government, rather it is linked to the lender's reversion rate – they can set that to whatever they want! Hence the ability to come out of this product whenever I wanted to with no penalties was imperative.

My solicitor was great and executed all the legal searches

and paperwork efficiently. He was ready to complete by the end of the month. The only thing holding us back was the mortgage offer. Since the new tax ruling, these few lenders that offer mortgages to limited companies were inundated with applications and suffering from huge backlogs. My broker advised that in order to expedite the process and send us to the front of the queue, we send the lender a signed letter from my solicitor stating that the mortgage offer was the only thing holding us back from completion. It worked. We completed end of March 2017, coinciding with my last day at Goldman Sachs.

I procured tenants at the full market rent of £950 pcm. After deducting the high mortgage repayment and the £10 a month buildings insurance I'd arranged, I was making an incremental £430 profit a month. Aside from the 15% deposit and the £8K spent on legal fees, stamp duty and mortgage fees, I again spent circa £2K getting the house prepared for rental. The cash amount required was £34K. I had £24K sitting in the company business account and loaned another £10K from my personal account to it.

Let's summarise the investment:

Property Six	
Purchase price	£160,000
Monthly rent	£950
	⇒ Gross yield 7%
Return On Investment	
Cash investment	£34,000
Annual profit[29]	£5,200
	⇒ ROI in 2017 was 15%
Payback Period	
Estimated payback period	7 years
Actual payback period	TBD
Equity released to date	£16,000
Remaining investment[30]	£12,000
	⇒ ROI in 2018 is 43%

The interesting thing to note with this investment is that my mortgage repayments are higher than my monthly profit. That means I have less of a buffer should interest rates rise. Again, the no early repayment charge feature is key here and means if interest rates shoot up and the rent no longer covers the interest repayment, I could remortgage to a lower LTV with lower interest repayments. Now, lowering the LTV is only feasible if the value of the property increases (unless one is willing to invest more money into

---

29 Since it is a freehold house, there are no service charges and ground rent to pay but there is buildings insurance.

30 In addition to the equity release, I have been earning rental profits from the property to pay back my cash investment.

the property), and this is where confidence around market values is necessary. I knew I was getting a good price on the house as similar properties were on the market for £180K+, and I also felt confident that barring a UK recession, the property value wouldn't really fall below £170K and definitely not £160K. And if a recession did take place, the UK government wouldn't be in a position to hike up interest rates anyway so the mortgage repayments would remain manageable. How one accumulates confidence around house price levels and negotiating the right price forms the content of Property Seven.

To conclude, let's pull out the key takeaways from this chapter:

✓ EXPLORE COMMUTER HUBS NEAR POPULATED CITIES
✓ USE VIEWINGS & AGENTS TO STUDY AREAS
✓ PAY ATTENTION TO EMPLOYMENT, SHOPS & SCHOOLS
✓ < ONE HOUR COMMUTE TO A LARGE CITY IS IDEAL
✓ WALKING DISTANCE TO A STATION INCREASES RENT
✓ USE THE EPC TO VERIFY PROPERTY CONSTRUCTION

PROPERTY SEVEN

NEGOTIATING THE RIGHT PRICE

If You Buy at the Right Price, It's Never a Bad Time to Buy

During the Milton Keynes transaction, I continued to simultaneously look for investment opportunities for my remaining £30K of rental income savings. In Property One and Two, I went over budget by £2K; budgeting now for no salary, I had to be precise with my numbers as there would shortly be no rolling corporate income to top me up! Assuming I could get another 85% LTV mortgage, I needed to buy something with a budget of £140K to ensure the £30K would suffice a 15% deposit, stamp duty, mortgage fees, legal fees, any subsequent renovation and the mortgage repayments while the place remained untenanted. I set my sights on Northampton.

Analogous to Milton Keynes where one had to be wary of non-standard construction properties, Northampton has many unsuspecting ex-council areas that do not look ex-council, but the rental demand is still considerably lower in these parts of town. Furthermore, a large proportion of houses in central Northampton have an unfamiliar layout, namely, the only bathroom and its single access is through the kitchen. It's something I hadn't come across before but quickly realised it is very much the norm in this area. I pictured tenants cooking in the kitchen, turning the extractor fan on that little bit louder to avoid hearing untoward noises emanating from the WC! Every time someone has a shower, do they need to run back and forth through the kitchen in a towel? I really felt this layout could curb rental demand and evidently, my concerns were shared as some of the houses on these roads that were notorious for this layout had actually changed it; they had turned one of the bedrooms upstairs into a second bathroom. That didn't work for me either, from a yield perspective, as the two-bedroom two-bathroom houses were still the same price as the three-bedroom ones.

I managed to find a purpose-built three-bedroom house with an upstairs bathroom, asking price £135K with an expected rent of £850 pcm, and a corresponding gross yield of 7.6%:

GROSS YIELD

$$\frac{\text{Annual Rent}}{\text{Purchase Price}} = \text{Gross Yield (\%)}$$

$$£10,200 / £135,000 = 7.6\%$$

A gross yield of 7.6% meant that I could in fact offer more

than the £135K asking price and still hit my hurdle rate. To be precise, I could offer up to £145,714:

MAXIMUM PURCHASE PRICE

$$\frac{\text{Annual Rent}}{\text{Hurdle Rate (\%)}} = \text{Maximum Purchase Price}$$

$$£10,200 / 7\% = £145,714$$

To reiterate, **the profit is in the buying** since you can control if/where/what you buy and for how much versus what the market value will be when you need to sell. I required more data points to help figure out the right price to offer.

After careful analysis of all the negotiations I had encountered to date, successful and failed, I concluded there are eight factors that are influential in determining the equilibrium purchase price. Offering too little can land you in a bidding war, and offering too much can secure the deal but you overpay; these factors can help pinpoint the correct price to offer.

Factor 1 – HURDLE RATE

We have already established that by setting your own hurdle rate, you can effectively set your maximum purchase price. Committing to your hurdle rate, therefore, gives you the upper end of your negotiation range. The question is, how low should you go?

⇒ Considering this factor alone, £145K seemed like a reasonable price to offer up to.

Factor 2 – *MARKET VALUE*

There is a 'house prices' search function on Zoopla that lists the achieved sale prices for properties in any given postcode. If you filter by 'last sold' and pay particular attention to the properties sold within the last 12–18 months, you can get a good idea of how prices in the area are trending and can extrapolate the current market value. Furthermore, there is sometimes a 'property history' feature that will give you more detail about and often pictures of the individual properties. This can further guide your valuation as characteristics like 'in need of modernisation' or 'recently refurbished' naturally have a bearing on the price that was ultimately paid. You can then corroborate your view by looking at asking prices of houses that are currently on the market. Typically one would always apply some sort of haircut to the asking price, but you will come to realise that all agencies deploy different marketing tactics:

- Some inflate prices more than others so that when you negotiate 10% off, you think you're getting a good deal.
- 'Offers in excess of' or OIEO should not stop you from putting in lower offers.

- Some go in with a low price and an open day to instigate a bidding war, and once buyers get attached to a property and/or their desire to 'win' takes the driver's seat, they tend to overpay.

This is why one needs to look at sold and asking prices to form a strong opinion on what the actual current market value is. If you struggle with this component and need validation, you can always purchase a valuation report for £19.95 at www.hometrack.com that provides a value range based on comparables. [Personally, I find this product particularly useful when considering a further advance and I want to corroborate my new and increased, usually punchy, valuation before paying the fees.]

⇒ I learned that in the last year, three-bedroom mid-terrace houses on the same street had sold for anywhere from £120K up to £135K, depending on the condition. The house I was interested in was fully renovated and a new combination boiler had just been installed. The house was ready to let. Asking prices on fully renovated houses ranged from £135K-£150K. Based on all of this, I set a ballpark current value of the property at £130K-£135K.

Factor 3 – *SELLER'S POSITION*
We touched on this in Property Two where one can take advantage of the seller's position and pay less than market

value for a quick sale. There are three main positions of the seller to look out for:

1. Liquidity constraint – for example, the property stands to get repossessed because the seller cannot afford mortgage repayments, or they need the sale proceeds to buy another property.
2. The property is empty – the seller is losing out on rental income while still paying a mortgage. Moreover, a vacant property is subject to squatters and vandalism so they would want to transfer the liability as soon as possible.
3. The property is a nuisance – e.g. the seller is moving country and wants the sale resolved before they leave.

⇒ #2 applied in my case: the property had recently been vacated, renovated, and the seller wanted a quick sale as she was now paying a mortgage without receiving any rent. I shaved £5K off the ballpark and figured she would settle at £125K-£130K in exchange for a quick transaction.

Factor 4 – BUYER'S POSITION
There are numerous reasons as to why a deal, once agreed, can still fall through. Aside from the seller pulling out, or something problematic being unearthed about the property that no longer makes it an attractive deal, the buyer's position can also slow down or block the sale:

1. The property is mortgageable but the buyer struggles to get financing because can't meet lending criteria, e.g. he or she has a poor credit rating.
2. The buyer is part of a chain and cannot complete the deal until they have sold a property.
3. The buyer is very slow in getting things moving, not getting documents to their broker or solicitor in a timely manner or at all.
4. The buyer plays games – for example, as the sale progresses they decide to renegotiate the purchase price for no good reason. It is important to state here that if there is a justified reason such as the lender has down valued the property, or during the legal process something has been uncovered that will cost like a major works bill that had not been declared, of course the buyer should renegotiate and with full confidence vis-à-vis the valuation report the bank will provide or the search results from the solicitor.
5. The buyer is fickle as to whether they want to proceed or keep looking for a better deal.

⇒ I was in a very strong position. My broker could confirm to the agent that my financing would not be a problem, which is an advantage of having a mortgage broker from a renowned firm in that their confirmation holds value. Being a buy to let investor, I wasn't part of a chain. I could demonstrate to the agent that I was on top of the process by immediately emailing him my proof of ID, proof of deposit, my company details and my solicitor's contact details. In addition to all of this, I would indicate that I'm always looking for investments so that they could view me as a future commission stream (agents get paid every time they sell a property). And finally, I would allude to using their lettings team to rent out my property – an additional revenue stream for their agency if they choose me. [Once you complete, you can let out the property through whoever gets you the most rent.] All in all, I could promise a quick transaction and therefore stuck to the ballpark of £125K-£130K.

Factor 5 – BUOYANCY OF MARKET

People often question if it's a good time to buy property or not, and they refer to the economic conditions and take a call on how they expect future prices to trend. But it is such a high-level generalisation that it almost becomes inconsequential. To buy what exactly? For example, while places like Luton have enjoyed significant capital growth, some parts of London have lost value during the same time period. Sometimes certain types of properties in a particular area stay on the market for a year, typically because prices in that area have plateaued but the sellers are adamant on getting the peak prices their neighbours achieved. Here you can often negotiate aggressively. Sometimes during the same period, properties in a different area and/or at different price points are flying off the shelves so to speak, indicating a growth area or an area that still offers relatively attractive yields. Here you often pay a premium to secure the deal. Shouldn't each area be considered on its own merit? In 2014, new stamp duty tax rules were enforced where a property that was bought for £400K for example saw a saving in the tax due, and a property bought for £2m demanded a significant increase in stamp duty tax. Now would you say that was a good time or a bad time to buy? It depends on the price point.

⇒ In this case, three-bedroom houses at the sub-£140K price point in Northampton were disappearing off the market daily. I was monitoring Zoopla every day, and literally in one instance two hours after it went live on the website, the agent told me an investor had called in, a viewing had been conducted, an offer had been made, negotiated on and accepted! In order to secure the deal, I upped my ballpark by £5K to £130K-£135K.

Factor 6 – ASPECTS THAT DEVALUE

Having gone through these in Property Three, essentially anything that requires a large cash outlay gives you a reason to discount the offer price, primarily:

- Substantial refurbishment requirements
- Unmortgageable so cash purchase only
- An upcoming section 20/major works bill (these need to be paid in full by landlords; owner-occupants can pay in instalments)

The more cash that is required, the more you can negotiate the price. And it shouldn't necessarily be 1:1. That means if there was a £10K major works bill attached to a property, I would discount my offer by more than £10K. Let's imagine a £300K flat and an identical flat in a different block for £290K but with a £10K section 20 served on it. Which would you rather buy? I would much rather buy the £300K to minimise my cash outlay: assuming a 25% deposit, I would need £75K cash for the £300K flat while the £290K flat would require a £72.5K deposit plus £10K cash for the major works bill. On a side note, one should also take into account when the next anticipated major works bill would be on the £300K flat. If no works had taken place on the block for a few years and were soon expected, I would be less aggressive in my effort to get a much larger than 1:1 discount.

⇒ None of the above applied to this property and I therefore stayed with the £130K-£135K ballpark.

Factor 7 – RENTAL STRESS TEST

Buy to let lenders have always undertaken affordability tests in order to get comfortable with a borrower's ability to repay a mortgage. In 2017, these affordability tests got much stricter. Most lenders used to require the rental income to cover at least 125% of the mortgage repayments (interest coverage ratio), and that too while assuming the mortgage repayment interest rate was 5% (stress test interest rate). If we use the last Milton Keynes property I bought as an example:

- Loan amount £136,000
- Stress testing at 5% implies repayments of £567 pcm
- Covering 125% means the rent requirement is £708 pcm

Per the rental stress test requirements, the lender required Property Six to rent out for at least £708 per month. The monthly rent I achieved was £950 pcm, nearly £250 over. However, these affordability levels have now increased from an interest coverage ratio of 125% and an interest rate of 5% to an average of 145% and 5.5% respectively.[31] Sticking with Property Six to illustrate, the specific lender I used had new levels that were even tighter than usual with an interest coverage ratio of 155% and a stress test interest rate of 6%! Under the new rules, the monthly rent required would have been:

- Loan amount £136,000
- Stress testing at 6% implies repayments of £680 pcm
- Covering 155% means the rent requirement is £1,054 pcm

Had the property been subjected to the new rules, it wouldn't have survived the lender's scrutiny. I would have been forced to borrow less by taking out a lower LTV product. The reason it wasn't subjected to the new rules is that the higher interest coverage ratio only applies to

---

31   Unless you are willing to fix your interest rate for five years as opposed to two or three, in which case there are some lenders that will soften these levels.

borrowers buying in their personal name while limited companies (for now) are still tested at 125%!

⇒ I applied the company stress test levels to the North-ampton property I was interested in, assuming a purchase price at my upper range of £135K and an LTV of 85%:

- Loan amount £114,750
- Stress testing at 6% implies repayments of £574 pcm
- Covering 125% means the rent requirement is £717 pcm

Given the expected rent for my prospective investment was £850 pcm, the property met the rental stress test. But then something occurred to me. Buying in a company is more expensive than buying in one's own name as I am paying higher interest rates on my company mortgages. Many interested investors would be buying in their own names and subjected to a higher interest coverage ratio. Applying the higher interest coverage ratio, the required monthly rent would be:

- Loan amount £114,750
- Stress testing at 6% implies repayments of £574 pcm
- Covering 155% means the rent requirement is £889 pcm

Performing similar calculations for an individual buyer, a purchase price of £130K would require £856 pcm in rent, and a purchase price of £125K would require £823 pcm in rent.[32] I figured that my ability to purchase in a company and the perks that came with that were advantages for me to capitalise on, not the seller. On this basis, and having incorporated a small buffer in case the surveyor down valued the expected rent on the valuation report, I reduced my maximum purchase price to £125K.

Factor 8 – BUDGET

In addition to the deposit, one needs to take into account all upfront costs including stamp duty, refurbishment costs, major works bills, mortgage costs and legal fees. Furthermore, the ongoing costs like mortgage repayments, insurance premium, ground rent, service charges, ad hoc maintenance and expected tax liabilities need to be assessed to ensure the rent will cover all of them and still produce a profit.

⇒ If I purchased at £125K with an 85% LTV mortgage, my upfront cash outlay would have been:

- £18,750 deposit
- £3,750 stamp duty
- £0 refurbishment
- £1,000 mortgage costs
- £1,500 legal fees

---

32 The rental stress test calculations are inbuilt into the Buying Property, Releasing Equity and Negotiating Price calculators, which are all available on the Buy To Let Loose app.

This totalled £25K and suited my £30K budget. With respect to the ongoing costs:

- £400 per month mortgage repayment
- £50 per month insurance and ad hoc maintenance (averaged out)
- £76 per month (estimated) tax liability, assuming 19% corporation tax

Assuming I'd achieve a market rent of £850 pcm, this still left a monthly profit of £324.[33] The maximum purchase price of £125K remained.

[You can use the Negotiating Price calculator on the Buy To Let Loose app that incorporates these eight factors and indicates the kind of offer you could make for a given property.]

It is human nature for all parties to strive for a good deal. If fair value is paid, neither party gets a good deal as such. In order for one party to have gotten a good deal, it by default means the other did not. The great thing about property is, the fair value can be debated using the eight factors discussed and so it is possible for both parties to *feel* as if they have gotten a good deal, and this is most easily

---

33   This calculation, including the estimated tax liability, is inbuilt into the Monthly Profit calculator on the Buy To Let Loose app.

achieved by meeting somewhere in the middle. Therefore, I generally offer around 5% less than the price I want to pay to allow room to work my way up, or in the eyes of the agent and the seller, to give in. Offering lower than that can absolutely work in a slow market where the seller is not receiving many offers, and you can negotiate over a few days to a few weeks even. However, in a buoyant market where properties are being snapped up as soon as they hit the market (and more often than not, before), lowballing your offer can take you out of the running as a non-serious buyer, or one that likes to play games.

I offered £120K. I put it in writing enclosing my ID, proof of deposit, my solicitor's contact details, an email attachment from my mortgage broker approving my financing, and an informal promise to complete within 6–8 weeks. I also added that I had other properties I was looking at and needed an answer ASAP. I concluded the email by stating that £120K was my final offer. The agent came back the same day and said the seller had rejected my offer, but that she would be willing to accept £128K. I immediately said no, that it was too high and that it wouldn't meet the rental stress tests of my lender. He then offered to speak to the seller again. He came back with £125K. I agreed on the basis that the deal was agreed that same day (to prevent the agent from shopping around for more offers) and that the property was immediately taken off the market.

I managed to secure the following mortgage product:

- 85% LTV
- Interest-only
- 4.39% variable (linked to the lender's standard variable rate)
- 25-year mortgage term
- £150 application fee
- £400 valuation fee
- 2.5% arrangement fee
- No early repayment charge (ERC)

It is useful to state here that the lender will value your property either at or below the purchase price. If they down value it, renegotiate the purchase price to the lender's value. If they value it at your purchase price, there is no need to feel that you haven't achieved a good price – the surveyor will never state a value above the purchase price, even if you are clearly buying below market value. If you want some assurance that you are indeed buying below market value, you can always commission an independent valuation for a completely objective report from the Royal Institution of Chartered Surveyors (RICS).

I loaned £25K to my company and completed the transaction. I didn't have to spend anything on renovating the house and managed to procure tenants at the full market rent of £850 pcm.

Let's summarise the investment:

Property Seven	
Purchase price	£125,000
Monthly rent	£850
	⇒ Gross yield 8%
Return On Investment	
Cash investment	£25,000
Annual profit	£5,300
	⇒ ROI in 2017 was 21%
Payback Period	
Estimated payback period	5 years
Actual payback period	TBD
Equity released to date	£0
Remaining investment[34]	£19,000
	⇒ ROI in 2018 is 28%

By analysing these eight factors, I negotiated with confidence and managed to obtain a great yielding investment. As much as I'd always like to get a bargain and buy below market value (BMV), it is important to keep opportunity cost in mind. That is the cost of not putting money to work. There are deals I have lost through negotiating too aggressively, and in hindsight, a couple of thousand pounds premium would have been recouped in a few months of rent anyway. Equally, one shouldn't buy a poor yielding investment out of frustration. I recently spent six months and £2K on a

---

34 I have been earning rental profits from the property to effectively reduce my cash investment.

transaction in Milton Keynes where we were one week away from exchange & completion. As usual, I went to inspect the property before I signed the contract, only to find the house had been vandalised! The seller hadn't disclosed this to their solicitor, and neither was he willing to pay for the damages. Tallying the additional £5K of costs needed, the deal no longer made sense for me. I pulled out of the transaction and accepted £2K of sunk costs, i.e. costs that are unrecoverable either way and therefore should not be taken into account when deciding whether to proceed with an investment.

Going forward, in order to maintain a strong buyer's position for future negotiations, I needed to identify which lenders of an already small pool of company-friendly ones would still be willing to lend to me given I no longer had a base salary. We will address this in the final case study, Property Eight.

To conclude, let's pull out the key takeaways from this chapter:

✓ USE HURDLE RATE TO SET MAXIMUM OFFER PRICE
✓ ESTABLISH MARKET VALUE TO REFINE YOUR OFFER
✓ FIND OUT SELLER'S POSITION
✓ LEVERAGE YOUR BUYING POSITION
✓ UNDERSTAND BUOYANCY OF THE SPECIFIC MARKET
✓ IDENTIFY ASPECTS THAT DETRACT VALUE
✓ RUN STRESS TEST SCENARIOS TO REFINE OFFER
✓ IF IT STILL FITS YOUR BUDGET, OFFER 5% LESS

PROPERTY EIGHT

CONTINUING WITHOUT A JOB ...

Have Your Ducks in a Row
So Your Portfolio Can Still Grow

Come June 2017 I was jobless, fully living off my rental income, and I had £5K of capital left to invest. Fortunately, it was time to remortgage Property Three. I stayed with the incumbent lender and had them revalue the property. From an initial 80% LTV, I switched to a 75% LTV product with a lower interest rate, thereby reducing my monthly mortgage repayments, and I released £30K.

With a fresh budget of £35K, I continued to look in Northampton since it suited my budget and I liked the yields it was still offering. I came across a property almost identical to Property Seven. And so, again, I offered £120K with a maximum purchase price of £125K in mind. We settled at £124K.

To recall, at the time there were thirteen lenders that accepted applications from companies:

1. Aldermore
2. Kent Reliance
3. Precise

4. Paragon
5. Metro Bank
6. National Counties Building Society
7. Axis
8. Shawbrook
9. Vida
10. Newbury Building Society
11. Buckinghamshire Building Society
12. State Bank of India
13. Fleet Mortgages

Most of these lenders required a minimum taxable income of £25K, and some of them required that it came solely from employment. A few of them had no minimum income requirement, but instead they required the company director to be an experienced landlord with several buy to let properties, and sometimes a residential one as well.

Given I was no longer employed, in order to assess my taxable income I needed to provide my SA302s (available to those that file self-assessment tax returns). My tax advisor sent me the requested documents for tax years ending 2014, 2015 and 2016.

I will take this opportunity to say, please hire a good tax advisor. I pay £240 a year to have all of this correctly documented and filed for me as I do not have the time to keep up with the ever-changing regulations. For example, as of September 2017, HMRC confirmed that they would no longer send agents paper copies of SA302s for mortgage application purposes. Most lenders apparently now accept 'tax overviews' and 'full calculations' – I wholly rely on my tax advisor to send me whatever my broker needs. Plus, a good tax advisor will understand all the ways in which one can legally keep taxable income as low as possible. The icing on the cake is, fees for tax advice are valid expenses that can be deducted. So if you are a higher rate taxpayer for example paying £240 a year for tax advice, you can claim 40% of that fee back from your tax liability; your effective tax advisor cost would be £144.

I opted for the following product:

- 80% LTV
- Interest-only
- 3.5% fixed for two years
- 25-year mortgage term
- £450 valuation fee & application fee
- 1.5% arrangement fee

I loaned the full £35K to my company and completed the transaction that summer. I procured tenants at the full market rent of £850 pcm, after spending £1K carpeting the whole house.

Let's summarise the investment:

Property Eight	
Purchase price	£124,000
Monthly rent	£850
	⇒ Gross yield 8%
Return On Investment	
Cash investment	£32,000
Annual profit	£6,600
	⇒ ROI in 2017 was 21%
Payback Period	
Estimated payback period	5 years
Actual payback period	TBD
Equity released to date	£0
Remaining investment[35]	£25,000
	⇒ ROI in 2018 is 26%

I should highlight here that these investment summaries, though rather tedious, are becoming increasingly critical to understand. As I write this, lenders are becoming stricter with buy to let portfolio applications in that many now require somewhat of a business plan: they want insight into your cash flow situation, how any shortfall in rent will cover the mortgage repayments, tenant profiling, how much rent is set aside for maintenance, how void periods are managed, etc. My advice is to read the corresponding lending criteria before submitting an application to avoid putting anything

---

35   I have been earning rental profits from the property to effectively reduce my cash investment.

controversial in the business plan – for instance, you plan to house council tenants when clear criteria of theirs preclude you from doing so. It sounds far more burdensome than it actually is and should take about fifteen minutes to fill out the additional paperwork, but it is important to at least understand the basic numbers behind your investment strategy. Ask your mortgage broker to guide you.

Two of the company mortgages I have are linked to standard variable rates, and having this product rate fixed was good in terms of spreading interest rate risk: with the outlook for interest rates now not as clear as it has been, it is prudent to manage the impact of an interest rate rise by spreading the risk over different types of mortgage products, and perhaps lenders too.

My buy to let growth strategy continues with equity having been released from the Milton Keynes house, and an upcoming release of equity from my residential home that is earmarked for an HMO (house in multiple occupation), which will allow me to rent each room out separately to increase the yield. I end this book here though because it is after Property Eight that I achieved what I sought out to do, and that was to earn enough passive income so that I could leave the corporate world behind and take control over my own time. I will reflect the level of financial security in the Conclusion, but I am grateful to say that anything going forward will simply be a bonus for me.

To conclude, let's pull out the key takeaways from this chapter:

✓ USE A TAX ADVISOR TO FILE ANNUAL RETURNS
✓ ACCRUE TWO YEARS OF SA302s BEFORE QUITTING
✓ CHECK YOUR TAXABLE INCOME IS OVER £25K
✓ IF NOT, OWN AT LEAST THREE BTL PROPERTIES ...
✓ ... AND IF POSSIBLE, A RESIDENTIAL ONE TOO
✓ DIVERSIFY MORTGAGE LENDERS IF POSSIBLE
✓ SPREAD INTEREST RATE RISK IF FORECAST IS VAGUE

CONCLUSION

CHOOSING A STRATEGY THAT SUITS YOU

There Are Multiple Roadmaps to Being FR££ – the Right One Depends on the Kind of Journey You Want to Have

I really admire the fearless few that can venture out there and do exactly what they want, taking a leap of faith that the money aspect will fall into place. Most of us, however, need a little handholding, and a passive income is a great safety bridge that can transcend a daunting leap into a very manageable stroll.

Everyone will have a level they need to hit in order to be financially secure – able to cover all necessary costs without a salary – and a somewhat higher level to feel financially free – able to cover luxury costs as well. My goal has always been to achieve financial security and to then use it as a platform to start my own business, which hopefully one day will lead to financial freedom. For those of you that would like to quit your day job and never worry about money or work again, you may choose to hold onto employment a little longer until your passive income surpasses financial security and approaches the financial freedom goalpost.

By summer 2017, the monthly profit generated by my property portfolio mirrored the net amount I used to get on my payslip every month. It was enough to cover all living costs and general spending that I could comfortably get by without a job per se. Coupled with the equity release I had gotten from capital appreciation in the last year alone of £164K (which equates to a gross cash bonus of £300K when on the payroll), yes I was pocketing more cash through property than I was in a corporate role. I had personally achieved financial security.

In addition to the rental income, my equity – the total value of all the properties in the portfolio less the total value of all the mortgages – across the eight properties was now in excess of £1m. In other words, if I were to sell the property portfolio at market value and pay off all the mortgages, I would be left with over £1m in cash.[36] To recall, I had managed to save £110K directly from my salary over the years while the rest had all come from rental income, releasing equity and reinvesting; the corporate world had enabled me to save £110K while property took that £110K of savings and turned it into £1m. This is a testament to property being able to make and save you more money than many corporate salaries.

When choosing the right level for you to give up the day job, other factors can also play a big part. Do you find balance in the lifestyle you lead? How much of your stress is driven by financial worry? Are you fulfilling your lifelong desires? A rental income that matched my salary, a residential home, £1m of savings and my time back to pursue whatever I wanted was more than enough for me to trade in the corporate world.

---

36   The sale proceeds would be subject to capital gains tax.

Do I Have to Invest, Why Can't I Just Save?

Firstly, any cash you hold in the bank is losing real wealth at current interest rates, thanks to an inflation level of 3%.[37] That means it is getting 3% more expensive to buy things every year. Let's say you put aside £5,000 every year to buy an annual travel card. Due to inflation, that annual travel card now costs £5,150. But your bank only gives you 1% interest so your £5,000 has only increased to £5,050. It hasn't kept up with inflation. In other words, so long as interest rates on savings are lower than inflation, any cash in the bank will continue to lose its purchasing power.

Secondly, **investing in income-generating assets is the only way to obtain true financial security**: a job you can lose and savings will deplete; even if you inherit significant wealth or win the lottery, if you continue to live off that money, eventually it will run out one day. The only way to stop it from spending down is to invest it wisely and live off the income it produces.

What Are the Alternatives to Investing in Property?

There are many paths to financial freedom – investing in property is merely one and not for everybody. Having worked in investment management for many years, I have experience across a multitude of assets including public equity (listed stocks), private equity (private businesses)

---

37   As of January 2018

and fixed income (bonds). I have seen individuals make and lose money across each of these asset classes. I have also witnessed people making obscene amounts of money very quickly with one-off investments: radically, anyone who invested £100 in the crypto-currency Bitcoin in 2010 and held onto it for seven years became a multi-millionaire! Not only are there many paths to financial freedom other than property, there are many shortcuts too. Generally speaking, the shorter paths are the riskiest and the one you take will depend on the type of journey you want to have.

Public equity/stock picking

Investing in single stocks can have a similar return profile to property. Like property, stocks can also rise significantly in a short period of time resulting in considerable capital appreciation. If you choose stocks with high dividend yields, you also receive income through dividend payments. The upside with stock investing is unlike property where the transaction fees are very high (stamp duty, legal fees, mortgage costs, etc.), the transaction fees for buying listed stocks are very low. Moreover, there is far less running around with stock picking: no viewings, no liaising with builders, tenants, solicitors, agents, and no maintenance required. The downsides are: you have no control over the dividend payments you'll receive and they are not guaranteed to stay at a prescribed level, unlike the rent levels which you can somewhat control; to borrow against a stock position is difficult unless you are a professional investor, and therefore you lose out on the power of leverage; and individual companies, no matter how big, are still more likely to go bust than an entire (developed) property market falling to £0... think Lehman Brothers whose shares became nearly worthless overnight![38]

With a post-graduate degree specialising in corporate finance and a career centred on investing cash under my belt, I am quite comfortable valuing companies and wanted to use this knowhow to create a separate revenue stream for myself. I invested £20K into ten AIM listed stocks[39] a few years ago that all had a 'strong buy' rating across several investment banks. Within one month, that £20K turned into £30K... two months on that £30K fell to £900... three years on, it's still sub-£1K and hasn't recovered. That's more than a 95% loss! Despite (or maybe because of!) my financial knowledge, I made some very wrong calls. Now if it had gone the other way, I could have doubled my money and made a quick £20K. But in order to make that kind of money quickly in the stock market, one has to be willing to lose that kind of money just as quickly. That loss completely put me off stock picking for life. But this is merely my personal experience and specific to single stock picking. To reduce the risk, one can buy a diversified portfolio of

---

38   Lehman Brothers, the fourth largest US investment bank at the time of its collapse, filed for bankruptcy on 15 September 2008.

39   AIM listed stocks are smaller companies whose price movements tend to be more volatile. This means you are more likely to make significant gains or losses in a shorter period of time. It is generally considered a more aggressive investment strategy than investing in larger companies listed on the FTSE 100 for example.

blue-chip stocks (generally household names like Apple, Vodafone, Coca-Cola). This is considered a much safer way to invest in public equities; refer to the 'Diversified investment portfolios' section for insight into taking a more balanced approach. Either way, I do believe the majority of people will find it easier to value a property by studying an area, recently sold prices, schools/restaurants/shops in the area and transport links versus taking a call on a company by studying industry dynamics, its balance sheet and monitoring key management changes.

Fixed income/bonds

Let's take government bonds of developed countries like the UK. Broadly speaking, you invest say £100 into a government bond, and so long as you hold it to maturity (a fixed term of two, five, ten years), you collect interest throughout the term and get your £100 back at the end. A lot more stable than equity dividends since the level of interest you'll receive is set, although the amount of interest on government bonds is very similar to that on a current bank account, negligible. This is because these government bonds are seen as risk-free investments since the UK government backs them; unless the UK defaults, you will get your money back at the end of the term. The difference between investing your money in government bonds versus holding it in cash is, during a downturn or a recession in the economy, some government bonds are seen as a flight to safety and the demand for them pushes up their value. For example during the financial crisis, UK government bonds increased in value by more than 10%. Essentially it's like putting your money into a savings account with the added bonus of getting some appreciation should the economy go belly up!

Then we get higher yielding bonds that pay more interest, generally 5%+. There are bonds issued by 'riskier' governments (reflected in a country's credit rating) like those of the emerging markets. They are definitely not seen as risk-free and offer high interest rates to compensate investors for taking the risk that the government could default on its payments... think Argentina, Venezuela. According to the Financial Times, Argentina has defaulted on its sovereign debt eight times since independence in 1816! With bonds issued by another country, you also take on currency and political risk. Then there are bonds issued by corporations that are effectively borrowing money from you and paying you interest. Corporations come with their own set of business specific and corporate governance risks; they can also declare bankruptcy and default on payments. Before the days of Netflix, do you remember spending Friday evenings browsing videos at Blockbuster? In 2010, Blockbuster missed interest payments to bondholders and later declared bankruptcy.[40] A rule of thumb is, the higher the interest rate promised to you, the higher the likelihood of default and the greater the risk to your investment.

---

40   Blockbuster filed for bankruptcy in the US on 23 September 2010.

Diversified/balanced investment portfolios

A prudent strategy that I used to advise clients of was asset diversification. It means to have a portion of savings allocated to government bonds, high yield bonds, public equity, and perhaps a portion allocated to private equity. I say prudent because this is a method for someone that wants to focus on capital preservation. Delving in deeper, the more focused on preserving capital that a client was, the larger the recommended allocation to developed country government bonds. The more appetite they had for growing their savings, and therefore taking on more risk, the larger the allocation to equity. However, so long as a client was diversifying assets, in a low-interest rate environment like the one we are in now, expected returns over the long-term were capped at circa 5% per annum. Growing savings by 5% every year is not going to grant us financial freedom! There's a saying in the investment world that goes like this: **"Concentrate your assets to get rich, diversify your assets to stay rich."** It means, pick an investment strategy and commit to it, be it investing in stocks, bonds, startups or property. It is indeed riskier but if you get it right, financial freedom will be achieved sooner. Once you reach a financial level that you are comfortable with, start to slowly diversify and turn your attention to preserving your savings. Put differently by Robert T. Kiyosaki in *Rich Dad Poor Dad*:

"If you have little money & you want to be rich, you must first be focused, not balanced. If you look at any successful person, at the start they were not balanced. Balanced people go nowhere. They stay in one spot. To make progress, you must first go unbalanced."

Real estate investment trusts

A real estate investment trust or a REIT is a company that owns income-generating properties, and investors can buy shares in the company and benefit from the income without having to themselves invest directly in property. What is most attractive about investing in REITs is one gets to invest in the property market without the hassle and costs of actually having to buy any. The reasons I prefer physical properties are: I can control the area, I can set the rent levels to meet my hurdle rate, and most importantly I am able to borrow money to increase my return on cash. By way of example, let's say I invest £25K cash in a REIT delivering 8% a year to its investors, that's £2K of income I get every year. Let's compare that to Property Seven that was also an 8% yielding investment where I invested £25K cash, but instead I get 8% on the full value of the property (£125K), that's £10K of income every year. Even after expenses, it translates to a 21% return on cash – all thanks to the power of leverage.

Private equity

Investing in private equity means to invest in private businesses that are not listed on a public exchange like the

London Stock Exchange.[41] Examples of private companies in the UK include John Lewis, Iceland and Virgin Atlantic.

Let's say you wanted to buy a stake in Buy To Let Loose – the book seems like it will do well, the app is gaining traction and you buy into its global expansion plan, that investors outside the UK will also want to learn more about property investing in the UK. You and I do a trade: you invest money in my business to help me grow it, and in return, I give you a 10% stake in the business. In a few years, the vision materialises and I sell Buy To Let Loose for a large amount of money. You get 10% of the sale proceeds and we both get rich! Or, Buy To Let Loose ends up being a great door stop in tens of houses, the app becomes redundant because a much bigger and better buy to let app becomes available, and post-Brexit people lose interest in investing in the UK. The only way to get out of the investment is if someone buys your stake from you; alas, no one wants it! Ten years on, I decide to wind up the business and your money goes with it.[42] This is private equity.

There are two ways to invest in private equity: directly, as explained above, or indirectly, through a private equity fund that invests in different private businesses and you invest in the fund. These private equity funds, though, are not easily accessible. The entry levels can start at £100K and sometimes much more, the fees are typically quite high,

41 For example, all FTSE 100 companies are listed on the London Stock Exchange (LSE) and are therefore not private businesses.

42 There are subsets of private equity investments that offer tax incentives. If you are interested in this asset class, please seek professional advice.

and investors tend to be institutional or of high net worth with considerable investment experience. In any case, direct or indirect, you would need to be prepared to have your money locked up for ten years plus.

Royalties, selling content, e-commerce

These options can feel a lot safer than outright cash investing because you end up substituting cash with time. For example, I am now selling content through this book and get paid a royalty every time someone buys it. This is also an example of generating passive income. But it has taken me time to create this content, to get a publisher, to create the supporting app – it's been a demanding job in itself and there is no way I would have been able to accomplish it while holding down full-time employment. I would recommend focusing on less time-consuming investment strategies while you have a solid day job, and perhaps transitioning into these forms of income generators once you have bought some time back.

These are some of the most common examples of income-generating investment strategies available to you. The investment strategy that is right for you will depend on your appetite for risk, the patience you have for the journey length, any views you have on and interests you have towards different markets, and potentially how easily accessible these various asset classes are to you.

I view buying property and renting them out as a

hybrid of bonds and equity. Like bonds, I also buy and hold property to maturity (the end of the mortgage term, typically twenty-five years), and so fluctuations in property prices do not affect me adversely, rather when they go up I release equity and when they go down, it's that much easier to identify and invest in more properties. I earn a fixed amount of monthly rent, similar to fixed income interest because it is contractually set, which is much more settling for me than seeing a public equity portfolio, in particular, gain and lose money on a day-to-day basis. Like equity though, property can also partake in considerable capital appreciation. The key differentiator is borrowing against property to reinvest is far more accessible for most people than borrowing against bonds and stock positions. And as demonstrated, leverage can be a useful tool for growing your passive income quickly.

Seven Advantages of Property Investing

1. Positive supply/demand dynamics

Despite concerns about net migration falling amidst Brexit, demand for housing outstrips supply and therefore property values continue to find support. According to the Office for National Statistics, the UK population continues to grow: the ONS says the population is projected to pass seventy million by mid-2029; in 2014 (pre-Brexit), they estimated that would happen by mid-2027. The point to draw out here is although the growth rate may have slowed down, and only partly due to a reduction in net immigration, our population is nonetheless growing and for housing to keep pace, the UK will need to build enough new homes to accommodate at least four more million people in the next ten years.

2. Potential for strong capital & income gain

You have two strong levers working for you, namely capital appreciation and income generation. Even when prices fluctuate, so long as you don't sell (or default on your mort-gage repayments), you won't lose the capital and all the while the rental income will continue to flow. And similarly, even if you suffer from rental void periods, you can still be 'making money' through capital appreciation.

3. Easier access to leverage

Let's say you put down £50K on a deposit for property. Borrowing £150K against a single buy to let is possible for many people, which is three times your cash investment. Whereas if you invest £50K into a single stock, to borrow even £20K against it – not even half – would be difficult and require a certain amount of investment experience, and a wealth profile that far exceeds what is needed for buy to let investing.

4. Good risk-adjusted returns

In what other asset class can you currently make a con-sistent 7–8% yield, and use leverage to increase that to 20% return on your cash, without taking on completely unmanageable risks? We refer to this as good risk-adjusted returns or asymmetric risk/reward, where the reward outweighs the risk.

5. Can buy below market value (BMV)

With property, one can buy below (or indeed above) market value whereas bonds, public equities and REITs have a standard market price. With a leeway in price thanks to the ability to negotiate, it is possible to already lock in some gains at the purchase point. You can buy a property with a built-in buffer knowing that even if the market price then goes down slightly, you'd still be up.

6. Shorter payback periods

Capital appreciation on property or equity is unpredictable compared to the income generated vis-à-vis rent or dividends. Focusing on the easier to forecast income generation, the payback period for property is much shorter than for equity, thanks to leverage. As we have seen through the case studies, one can earn back their investment on a property within a few years through the rental income alone (ignoring equity releases). Whereas even a high-dividend stock paying 5% per annum would take twenty years to earn the investment back through the income alone. The key is leverage and as discussed, borrowing against property is far simpler for the majority of the population. Therefore property investments typically much sooner pay back initial cash investments and reach the infinity

ROI stage – zero money continuing to make money. [Refer towards the end of Property One for a detailed explanation of infinity ROI.]

7. Relative stability

The price movement in UK property is relatively slow moving and the cash flow is fairly stable (so long as you've accrued properties that people want to live in). A strong and secure foundation, that isn't potentially compromised every morning when the markets open, can provide comfort and support to venture onto riskier pastures like investing in other people's startups, or indeed your own.

Seven Risks Of Property Investing & How I Manage Them

1. Fall in house prices

A fall in house prices coupled with a need to sell a property to meet a liquidity need could see you at a loss. I kept a day job to cover all liquidity needs until I was financially set up to fully sustain myself. I now have enough rent coming in to cover all costs and then some. This enables me to deploy a buy-to-hold strategy: I'm not reliant on prices staying high, as I have no need to sell, so I can actually use a fall in house prices to my advantage by finding cheaper opportunities to put more savings to work.

2. *Fall in rental demand and void periods*

A fall in rental prices or void periods can make it difficult for one to cover mortgage repayments. I buy in locations that have strong rental demand, and those usually are ones that are easily accessible to a central city – walking distance to a main station, within an hour's commute to London (when outside the capital) – and I avoid locations that have dozens of 'for let' signs up that can indicate soft rental demand (unless it's a student area and summer time!).

3. *Increase in interest rates*

An increase in UK interest rates probably means an immediate rise in mortgage repayments for variable interest products (depending on what the rate is linked to), and an inevitable rise once the fixed products end. This can reduce profits or force landlords to increase rents making their properties less attractive. I have been fortunate to have only invested in a low-interest rate environment. As the forecast becomes a little less clear, or rather veers towards the end of an era, I am diversifying lenders, varying products between fixed and variable, and I am slowly lowering the LTVs of the existing properties I have to ensure enough of a cushion between the rent I accrue and the corresponding mortgage repayment. What I do feel strongly about is this: once interest rates rise, indicating a healthier economy, so long as I can ride the increased payments out over the short term, inflation is sure to follow (if it isn't indeed the catalyst for interest rates rising). With inflation comes an increase in property values and rent. With increasing property values, the LTVs reduce and counter the impact of the interest rate hikes, as does the increase in rent.

4. Evicting tenants

Tenants can default on rent payments, forcing the landlord to evict them. This process can take at least six months, and that means six months of no rent and ongoing mortgage repayments. This is one of the two hardest risks to mitigate. In a nutshell, I vet tenants myself and direct debit rent to my account so that I can monitor all cash flows. This book is centred on the investing side of buy to let and assumes one would similarly outsource the rest to an estate agency for example. If you would like to take a very hands-on approach, there are several books on the market that educate us on creating tenancy agreements, finding good tenants, managing tenancies and dealing with evictions.

5. Empty properties

Empty properties (either between exchange and completion or while trying to find tenants) are subject to squatters. If squatters take up residence in an empty property, there is a legal process that needs to be enacted to remove them, which again could mean months of no rent. Empty properties are also subject to increased vandalism. When buying investment properties, I habitually exchange and complete on the same day, and the day before that I go and see the property to ensure all is in order. I also start informally marketing the property a couple of weeks before completion. This requires one to build a good relationship with the estate agent so that he or she can provide access for viewings.

6. Emigration

A reversal of the current inward flow of migration into the UK, in lieu of Brexit and certain tax laws, would reduce pressure on housing and shift the positive supply/demand dynamics. This would decrease property values and rental demand. I have already personally witnessed a few higher rate taxpayers leaving the UK, and several more are considering it if individual tax rulings become less favourable. Therefore, I deliberately build a portfolio of buy to let properties that target low-income households.

7. Increase in tax

The government increasing taxes on buy to let properties under an individual name or owned in a company. This is the second of the two hardest risks to mitigate. All I can suggest here is to have a good tax advisor on board that will have far better insight into the future. One of the main reasons mine advised me to set up a company is that corporation tax has been trending downwards in the UK. At the Summer Budget 2015, it was announced that corporation tax would be set at 19% for tax years starting April 2017, 2018 and 2019, and 18% from April 2020. Then in 2016, it was announced that from April 2020, the rate would reduce from 18% to 17%. Conversely, with serious talks of wealth tax being introduced in the UK, and higher and additional rate taxpayers being subjected to increasing income tax, the argument for continuing to invest in your personal name weakens. Importantly, future tax rulings can come into play for any asset class, not just for property, e.g. new dividend tax rulings could affect those with equity portfolios. Although having said that, targeting landlords has been the flavour of the month for the last four years running!

The key question that most of you will be asking yourselves is – have you missed the boat on property investing? And in my opinion, it's a resounding, not at all. People have been investing in property long before I have and would have argued that I had missed the boat. In fact, I could have argued that I had well ridden the curve by 2014 and gracefully bowed out after the significant equity release, only made possible due to the substantial increase in property prices in London. But the last four out of the eight case studies were 2017 purchases, all still surpassing my 7% hurdle rate.

Property investing is still very much a relevant strategy, despite continued efforts by the government to find new ways to tax profits, and I continue to heavily allocate my savings to the asset class. Going back to the lesson we learned in Property Seven – 'if you buy at the right price, it's never a bad time to buy' – we broke down the property market by areas and price brackets. And so, we can absolutely say we have missed the boat on certain specific markets, but on the whole property market? Not by a long shot. I will go as far as to say, yes, it is virtually impossible to source 7% yielding properties in London without increasing the number of bedrooms. And finding those opportunities are not easy. I mentioned in Property Eight that I am undergoing an HMO project in London currently, where I intend to turn a three-bedroom house into a five-room property (with the correct licensing in place). An easier route though, I feel, is the one I took of investing in commuter hubs. Now, Milton Keynes and Northampton have risen in value since I bought and currently outright purchases do not yield 7%. So what options do you have? Well, you could identify properties still in those areas and increase the number of bedrooms, like I did with Property Three. Or, Milton Keynes and Northampton are both within an hour north of London – how about exploring east, west or south of London? How about commuter hubs neighbouring Birmingham, Manchester, or indeed looking first in the suburbs of those cities? Will I end up buying in Northern Ireland in the foreseeable future? Perhaps. Or, as I had to learn all about the HMO licenses across different boroughs in London in an effort to get creative for Property X, should I similarly learn the rules of the road for buy to let in Scotland?

Property investing will continue to be attractive to me so long as it continues to offer appealing yields. The fact that the areas offering high yields don't stay hot for long should paint you a positive picture; property values can only rise when there is demand, and investors are snapping up all of the 7%+ opportunities. Finding the next wave of high-yielding opportunities means you need to be among the first batch hitting the area. It takes time and perseverance: surfing Zoopla replaces Snapchat downtime, estate agents become your new best friends, and taking trains to explore unchartered towns you've never heard of becomes the highlight of your weekend. Because in which other asset class can you easily access and fix these sorts of returns?

Whichever investment route you choose to embark on, you will also need to set the pace. I chose to leverage my properties and release equity at every opportunity I had, I decided to not pay off my MBA loan and reinvested the money instead, I chose to not contribute to my pension as I believed I could better invest the money myself, and I took out a personal loan from my bank. Some of you may feel I have borrowed aggressively and put all of my eggs into one basket, and some of you may feel I could have picked up the pace by borrowing from friends & family, partnering with investors, etc. This book is simply my experience pertaining to my risk appetite, preferences & biases, and skewed towards the level of financial freedom that suits me, written to hopefully encourage rather than prescribe.

It delights me to say that I now have time to dedicate to my own venture, and of course, to writing this book – I feel blessed that my investments have granted me the freedom to complete it.

A final thought I will leave you with is, structurally we

are moving to a place where nothing is guaranteed. For example, when autonomous cars take over this world, what will happen to the millions of taxi drivers? With job automation on the rise, many industries will go out of fashion. Take a good look at public companies and private businesses – who knows what will survive and what won't in even ten years time! But, one will always need somewhere to live. And the land we have on this planet is finite.

GLOSSARY

Base Rate
This is the rate at which the Bank of England will lend money to commercial banks. When the UK economy refers to low interest rates, they are referring to the base rate.

Completion
Once you complete on a property, you are the legal owner. In order to complete, the lender will release the funds to your solicitor who will then send them to the seller's solicitor, assuming all legal queries have been satisfied and all documentation is in order.

Compulsory Purchase Order (CPO)
A public body can force you to sell them your ex-council property at market price. This can happen, for example, if an area is undergoing regeneration.

Early Repayment Charge (ERC)
Per your mortgage offer, there will be a fixed period that your mortgage product runs for before reverting to the lender's reversion rate. If you pay back your mortgage early or try to remortgage within that period, there could be a monetary penalty. This information can be found in the key facts illustration that your broker will provide you with, which you should receive and review before committing to taking out any mortgage.

Equity

This is the value of a property that belongs to you. For example, if you buy a property for £100K and have a £75K mortgage against it, your equity is £25K. If the value of the property increases by £100K (and your loan amount remains at £75K), your equity also increases by £100K. It is different to your investment in the property, which in this case is £25K.

Exchange

Exchange of contracts means there is now a legally binding agreement in place between the seller and the buyer on a property, confirmed with the buyer usually paying 10% of the purchase price.

Ex-Local Authority

Refers to properties that used to be owned by the local council, hence ex-council/local, and rented out to tenants that were of low-income households. Under Thatcher's government, a new housing act allowed these tenants to buy the council homes at heavily discounted prices, giving them the 'Right to Buy', and therefore created a wave of ex-council homes. Similar terminology is the Projects in the US.

Freehold

Permanent ownership of the land the property is built upon.

Hurdle Rate

The minimum gross annual return you would like the rental investment to achieve.

Investment

The amount of cash you have invested in the property. The investment will be your initial cash outlay upon purchasing the property. Your investment in the property will decrease as you earn rental profits and release equity to recoup your investment money, and it will increase if you put more money into the property. It is different to your equity in the property.

Key Facts Illustration

This is a document that will be provided to you by your mortgage broker, or directly by the lender if you are not using an intermediary. It outlines the mortgage product, all fees that will be incurred including early repayment charges, the monthly repayments you would be committing to if you take on the mortgage, and illustrations of what would happen to those repayments if interest rates were to rise.

Leasehold

Temporary right to lease the land the property is built upon, stipulated by the remaining number of years on the lease.

Lender's Interest Coverage Ratio (ICR)

Lenders require investment properties to demand enough rent that will not only cover the monthly mortgage repayment, but will also provide a significant buffer in case there is a shortfall in rent due to void periods or maintenance costs. 145% is currently the average interest coverage ratio.

Lender's Stress Test Interest Rate

Lenders require investment properties to demand enough rent that will not only cover the monthly mortgage repayment, but will also provide a significant buffer in case interest rates rise and the monthly repayments become more expensive. 5.5% is currently the average interest rate at which lenders stress test.

Leverage

Borrowing money.

Loan-To-Value

The percentage of the purchase price you would like to borrow. For example, if a property is worth £100K and you take out a £75K mortgage, this represents a 75% loan-to-value.

Marriage Value

A flat with a long lease is more valuable than a flat with a short lease. If a lease is renewed, the corresponding flat rises in value. Marriage value is half that increase in value and becomes payable when the lease being renewed is less than eighty years.

Passive Income

Cash flow received on a regular basis without actively working, e.g. rental income, royalties, dividends from stock positions.

Stamp Duty Land Tax (SDLT)

A tax set by the UK government that one has to pay when purchasing a property.

FORMULAS

GROSS YIELD

$$\frac{\text{Annual Rent}}{\text{Purchase Price}} = \text{Gross Yield (\%)}$$

MAXIMUM PURCHASE PRICE

$$\frac{\text{Annual Rent}}{\text{Hurdle Rate (\%)}} = \text{Maximum Purchase Price}$$

MINIMUM RENT REQUIRED

Purchase Price x Hurdle Rate (%) = Minimum Annual Rent

MONTHLY MORTGAGE REPAYMENT

$$\frac{\text{Loan Amount}}{12} \times \text{Interest Rate (\%)} = \text{Mortgage Repayment}$$

RETURN ON INVESTMENT (ROI)

$$\frac{\text{Annual Profit}}{\text{Cash Invested}} = \text{Return On Investment (\%)}$$

PAYBACK PERIOD

$$\frac{\text{Cash Invested}}{\text{Annual Profit}} = \text{Payback Period (years)}$$

USEFUL LINKS

Buy To Let Calculators   www.buytoletloose.com

Property Search   www.zoopla.co.uk
www.rightmove.co.uk

Property Valuation Reports   www.hometrack.com
www.ricsfirms.com

Market Rents   www.home.co.uk

Government Guidance   www.gov.uk/browse/
housing-local-services

Mortgage Brokers   www.alexanderhall.co.uk
www.charcol.co.uk

National Landlords Association   www.landlords.org.uk